'*Missing Christopher* is a faultless gaze into the heart... grief and love are enduring companions.'

—Patti Miller, author of *Writing Your Life* and *The Memoir Book*

'Jayne is clearly a superb writer . . . and she has produced a book that will be accorded "classic" status.'

—From the Afterword by Professor Gordon Parker

Rhonna,

missing christopher

with all my love

Jayne x

jayne newling

Afterword by
Professor Gordon Parker AO

Published with the assistance of the Black Dog Institute
www.blackdoginstitute.org.au

First published in 2014

Copyright © Jayne Newling 2014

All rights reserved. No part of this book may be reproduced or transmitted in any form or by any means, electronic or mechanical, including photocopying, recording or by any information storage and retrieval system, without prior permission in writing from the publisher. The Australian *Copyright Act 1968* (the Act) allows a maximum of one chapter or 10 per cent of this book, whichever is the greater, to be photocopied by any educational institution for its educational purposes provided that the educational institution (or body that administers it) has given a remuneration notice to the Copyright Agency (Australia) under the Act.

Allen & Unwin
83 Alexander Street
Crows Nest NSW 2065
Australia
Phone: (61 2) 8425 0100
Email: info@allenandunwin.com
Web: www.allenandunwin.com

Cataloguing-in-Publication details are available
from the National Library of Australia
www.trove.nla.gov.au

ISBN 978 1 76011 044 4

The names of some people in this book have been changed.

'All You Who Sleep Tonight' by Vikram Seth, © Vikram Seth, 1990. Reproduced by permission of Sheil Land Associates Ltd.

The poem by Nancye Sims is reproduced by permission of the poet.

The Cruelest Death: The enigma of adolescent suicide by David Lester © Charles Press, Philadelphia, PA, 1993

Set in 11.5/18 pt Legacy serif by Midland Typesetters, Australia
Printed and bound in Australia by Griffin Press

10 9 8 7 6 5 4 3 2 1

The paper in this book is FSC® certified. FSC® promotes environmentally responsible, socially beneficial and economically viable management of the world's forests.

Dedicated to Phil, Ben, Nic, Zach and Christopher (Cricket)

For of all sad words of tongue and pen,
The saddest are these: it might have been!

JOHN GREENLEAF WHITTIER

'Jayne's use of language is exquisite, creative and courageous. Her journey through grief is enveloping, harrowing, even excruciating at times, at others poignant and revealing. There is very little respite from the unrelenting anguish and agony of her grief.

'When you embark on the journey with Jayne, you find that survival is the task, as any of life's meaning seems to have died with Christopher until the birth of her precious grandson rekindles hope and pulls her back into life.

'This is a book which needs to be read by all who come into contact with, or care for, anyone experiencing complicated grief, whether as a family member or friend. Most importantly, for any mental health practitioner it is a must read.'

—Mal McKissock OAM
Co-Director, Bereavement Care Centre,
and author of *Coping with Grief*

part one

chapter 1

Overlooking the edge of the cliff from where my seventeen-year-old son died, I watched as a blond-haired toddler ran towards his mother and screamed. He had fallen and grazed his knees ten metres below, on the same rock Christopher's body thumped and splintered. The boy's white T-shirt was stained with red splotches, remnants of an icy-pole treat perhaps, and his blue tracksuit pants were split at the knee which he held with both pudgy hands as his mother tried to inspect the damage. She picked him up and carried him to the warm sand. I walked down the pathway, past the picnic bench and the now-consoled toddler who was distracted by his bucket and spade.

Large boulders formed a barrier between the cliff and the beach. Beyond, where the waves crashed over the rock pool at high tide, a high mesh fence protected bathers from falling rocks.

I knelt down to the rock for evidence of the toddler's blood. There was nothing but the indent of my son's broken body and if I closed my eyes, all I saw was blood gushing from his cracked skull into the black ocean, his right leg bent back, snapped in two. I saw a girl cradling his head with his favourite cream woollen jumper, begging him to open his eyes. I saw myself hyperventilating and restrained behind the fence by a policewoman. She shoved a brown paper bag over my nose and mouth and held it there against my will and ordered me to breathe deeply. I saw paramedics lifting my little boy onto a spinal board. I felt nothing. I heard nothing.

～

That was eleven years ago. I can now say my son is dead. I used to say we lost him, as though he was caught in some ephemeral haze and we were waiting for it to dissipate before he could be reunited into our family fold.

I used to say, when asked, that I have two children, as if Christopher, bookended by Ben and Nic, never existed. Then I tried saying three, to see if that was easier on my heart. I'd say Ben's the eldest and Nic's the baby and state their ages.

'And the middle one?' they would ask.

My heart would plummet and my eyes would throb with the weight of hot tears.

He's dead. That's it. There is no going back—except in my head.

In my head Christopher is now twenty-eight. I know what he looks like because his best friend, Ben 'Murgy' Murgatroyd, still comes to see me and they are like twins. They have the same shade of blond hair and their eyes are the blue on a kookaburra's wing. They have the same muscular frame and tanned skin and they smile with just enough teeth to be alluring. They both light up a room.

In my head Christopher hasn't married yet. He wants to ensure he picks the right one. He's in between jobs, surfing with Murgy in Bali.

He is much happier now. He isn't frightened his depression will turn him into a freak. He is now a man, confident and self-assured, not the teenager who hid his fears from friends and family. He is not the boy who gambled with life and lost.

In my head I am home on the night he drives to the southern end of Avalon beach on Sydney's Northern Beaches, kicks his car mirror and throws it and his mobile phone over the cliff. We are sitting in the kitchen drinking a cup of hot chocolate.

He is crying and I kiss the brown birthmark on his neck. He isn't drunk and angry but sad and quiet. We speak in whispers. His fears, once expressed, evanesce into the four walls surrounding us. He goes to bed. I mould the doona into the undulations of his tall and lean frame and stroke the thickening stubble on his cheek until he falls asleep. And in my head he is there in the morning, dressed for school, eating a large plate of bacon and eggs with sourdough toast and baked beans.

That was me then. Eleven years ago before I lost my son. There was always tomorrow and it didn't matter how hard life was, my husband Phil and I could survive anything. We'd been together since high school and our love was strong—we were still best friends. Even when Ben developed depression at sixteen and hid in his room for six months, followed shortly after by Nic who saw the walls moving in and wanted to kill people, we worked together to try to free our children's minds. Then, several months later, Christopher went off the rails and the impact was like someone had thrown a Molotov cocktail into our living room.

There's another place in my head which I never talk about. If I do, I fear I'll have to live there, forever. But it's there—just for me, like a dormant cancer cell waiting to splay its tentacles. It takes over me, paints me black and smells of bleach. It's insidious and it's always there behind my sane veneer, pretending to be padlocked by time. In this place I see a little boy trapped on a train.

He is screaming, tears falling in rivulets down his reddened, crushed face. His tiny fists bang soundlessly on the window. I'm on the platform running to jump on but as I do, the door closes. The train goes round and round a circular track and with each circuit the boy loses energy until he is no longer there.

And in this same place, his grown body is plummeting through the cold, dark air. There is no moon, there are no stars. The only illumination is the twinkling of streetlights across the beach to the next headland.

He is on his back, an inverted parachute, arms and legs to the heavens. He falls past his dented car mirror and the many parts of his shattered phone dot the precipice like jewels. Jagged rocks fly by; an errant dandelion, closed for the night, bows to the sudden disturbance, and the black mass of concrete and sandstone waits.

How long would it take? What was he thinking? Did he change his mind? Was he scared? I know he hated the dark.

In this place it is my fault. I didn't love enough, listen enough, care enough. There are no beautiful memories here. In this place, I am forced to go back to that Thursday night in August 2002, and watch my son die over and over and over again—in slow motion.

It was just before midnight. It was dark and I could just see the ghostly outline of a woman standing on a rock, purging herself in regular spasms, gagging like an injured animal.

Phil and I ran to the only light we could see, a dim torch by the ocean pool at the southern corner of the beach. A policewoman grabbed me and forced me to sit down. Her grasp was like a handcuff and I squirmed against her power. She was stronger than me. I looked at Phil beseechingly but all I saw was the terror mirrored in his own eyes and it scared me to death. We were separated from our son by the 3-metre mesh fence. I couldn't see him but I heard his two friends yelling against the crash of the waves. I was angry they were allowed to be there and not us. He was our son. I broke free and darted around the fence.

Christopher was lying on his back. There were six people encircling him. Ally, the sixteen-year-old girl he was living with, was cradling his head and his close friend Jack was highly agitated as he stared over the curved backs of the paramedics. Phil and I couldn't get through the human barrier.

The late night silence was broken by huge and unrelenting waves as they crashed over all of them. Someone screamed 'Fuck!' I wanted to go to my son but was held back again. I could feel someone grabbing at my tracksuit top and I pulled away.

Suddenly it was whisper quiet. I was looking down at my son but it wasn't real. There was an aura, a haze which was surreal and cold. I felt as if I was floating over the crowd, watching dispassionately as they tried to repair my son. There was a huddle of backs and a lone torch shining a dull ring of light on Christopher's chest. A loud wave suddenly crashed over the pool, the foam like dirty dishwater pooled around him. His body rocked with each new wave. He must have been so cold. I had to find a blanket.

Phil clutched my shoulder as we watched them gently manoeuvre Christopher onto a spinal board. I felt calmer now that they had lifted him out of the cold water. Phil knew our son was going to die but said nothing to me except that he was very thirsty and needed to find water. We walked behind the paramedics up to the car park where the ambulance waited. No one was in a hurry. That was a good sign. He was probably just concussed.

A policeman told us a helicopter had been called. Why? Couldn't they wake him up in the ambulance? My heart was still pounding but I felt sure this would be just another angst-filled night, one of many we'd endured over the years. By morning we'd be thanking the god I didn't believe in, the same god who would later give me constant headaches at the exact spot where my son's head cracked open.

Phil and I hurriedly arranged that I would go in the helicopter and he would go home to Nic, our fifteen-year-old asleep and alone just a few kilometres away; eighteen-year-old Ben was staying overnight at a friend's place. We waited outside the open doors of the ambulance. The car park was dark except for the warm glow casting halos inside the cavern of the makeshift intensive care unit. Word had spread and a group of Christopher's friends and parents stood in a huddle on a grassy mound by the picnic table.

I was waiting for breath, mine and his. The paramedics bent and straightened, moving from equipment to Christopher who was still lying on the spinal board. I couldn't see his face. They were methodical but busy. I saw bloodied cloths, plastic tubes and syringes. My heart had stopped. I was waiting to hear the roar of the helicopter. Why was it taking so long?

Then I heard it—in the distance. I touched Phil's arm but there was no reaction.

His head was bent, staring down at the tarred surface; he must have been really thirsty now. The roar was getting louder. I looked up to the headland, up higher to the imagined flight path. Louder, louder. I looked back into the ambulance. The frenetic activity had slowed. The dark sky had quietened. I pricked my ears. I couldn't hear the helicopter.

'Where's the helicopter?' I yelled out. A policeman grabbed hold of my elbow.

'They've turned it around,' he said. 'It's not needed anymore.'

Thank God. He was awake. He was okay. I crossed my fingers hoping whoever was calling the shots would also spare his legs. He had an important rugby match on Saturday. I smiled as a paramedic offered a big hand and pulled me up into the ambulance. I wanted to hug him. I was already thinking about what gifts I could buy for them. I would also donate money to the ambulance service. As I stepped in I wondered why Phil wasn't behind me. I still couldn't see Christopher. Two paramedics crouched over him. No one looked at me.

'Cricket?' I whispered.

That was his nickname. Everyone called him Cricket. When he was born, Ben called him Cricketer, unable to pronounce Christopher, and it was thereafter shortened to Cricket.

The paramedic let go of my hand and whispered something I couldn't hear. I didn't care, I just wanted to go to my son. As I neared, they stood aside. Their heads were shaking slowly and they stared at the floor. I panicked. Why weren't they smiling? Why weren't they happy and relieved? Why weren't they looking at me?

The tubes were gone and his arms lay inertly by his sides. His eyes were closed and his face was as white as an eggshell. Blood was matted in his hair and despite their efforts to 'present' him, red smudges stained his ears and neck and wet blotches marked the sheet under his head. His body was covered to his chest except for one shoeless foot which poked out from beneath the blanket.

No!

My brain snapped silently. I felt the blood drain from my head, down my body and out through the holes in the rubber soles of my ugg boots. I bent down to whisper I love you in his blood-encrusted ear. I kissed the birthmark on his neck and then his cold lips.

I looked over at the paramedics just in case I had made a mistake but they were busy throwing out the used syringes and tubes. I was shaking as I stared at them, wondering what to do. One paramedic saw my panic and helped me down the steps as Phil climbed into the cabin. I couldn't meet my husband's eyes.

I felt my heart break. It leaked through me like Christopher's had through the jagged and sharp edges of his broken rib cage. I heard my mind explode.

I was the ghost who walked away. Soulless, lifeless. The essence of me stayed behind with him—my son. Life ended there, in the ambulance, in that car park, in this world, and I forgot to say goodbye.

chapter 2

I hate goodbyes. Being with someone, especially my sons, and then alone. I wait till the last minute, stretch my neck through a door, around a corner, to prolong the dying moments. I wave frantically as Ben or Nic reverse out of our driveway back to their own homes. I'm still standing on the kerb as their tail lights disappear beyond the last pine tree. I never say the last goodbye.

When the boys were young and I had to go to work as a freelance journalist, one of them would always beg me to stay. I'd kiss and tickle them to make them laugh but feel the pull of guilt and loss as I drove away, their three sad faces staring out at me from the glass balcony doors, their little hands waving with little enthusiasm. Ben and Nic were stoic and, even though I left them with Deby, a close friend whom they all loved, Christopher always cried.

I couldn't wait to get home. I'd honk the horn, run up the stairs and scream 'hello' as they fought to be the first into my outstretched arms. We played for the rest of the day and went through the rituals of bedtime: dinner, bath, reading and then the Street Light Man. We'd huddle by the glass doors, our breaths making a canvas for creative fingers as we stared at the street lamp across the road. Then we'd sing our practised song: 'Come on Street Light Man, turn the street light on … Come on Street Light Man, turn the street light on … boom, boom boom.'

After several choruses, the lamp would light and the boys would ooh and ah. Magic.

~

We lived in a small two-bedroom weatherboard cottage in Bilgola on Sydney's Northern Beaches. Born close together, three under four, my sons slept in the same room on a triple bunk bed. Ben with Mickey Mouse on the top, Christopher with Bunny in the middle, and Nic with Clowny on the bottom. I'd tuck them all in, then sing a lullaby. It took forever to say goodnight, they fighting sleep, me not wanting to be alone. Phil, a wool buyer, was always home on weekends but away three out of four weeks. I missed him when the house was quiet, except when I had to write up my interviews, which I did while the boys slept.

When Nic was born, Christopher, who was 21 months old, was jealous of the new, squishy, demanding lump. He patted him like a dog and would rock his cradle at a speed worthy of an Olympic rower. He was not impressed by the constant feeding and burping and would try to climb up onto my lap when I breastfed. Finding the space fully occupied by his huge four-and-a-half-kilo (ten pound) brother he would wriggle with a grunt to the spot on the couch next to me, but not before throwing a possessive leg over my knee.

At bedtime after the nightly book-reading, song-singing rituals and when Phil was home, we would tippy-toe out of their room but we wouldn't get to the door before Christopher called us back. He always wanted another kiss. I would softly pinch his cheeks while rubbing my nose against his.

'Moochie, moochie,' I'd say.

'Moochie, moochie, Mama.'

Only then would he turn his chubby little body to the wall, hugging Bunny around his face. We'd finally leave to the sound of him sucking his thumb while twirling Bunny's silken tag around his ear.

∼

The next day we'd play in the park or at the beach. When Ben started preschool we'd all stand at the gate waving wild goodbyes. As he turned the corner, we'd all run in to give him one last hug. Christopher cried when it was his turn to go to school. It didn't matter how many goodbyes, he always begged for another one. Nic was more assured. One goodbye and a wave of his hand was all he needed.

They all went to the same primary school, a short walk from home. Ben was a big boy when he started and strode up the path without a backward glance. When it was Nic's turn, he held on to his best friend Simon's hand. But Christopher lingered as long as he could before letting go of my thumb and with a bowed head he'd trudge up the driveway, turning around every few seconds for one last look. I missed them, too. I was a canteen mother once a week so I could catch glimpses of them in the playground. I'd sneak treats out to them when the other duty mothers were occupied with meat pies or lolly bags. The boys would giggle conspiratorially then rush off to share their goodies with friends. Each term I alternated between their classrooms, taking groups for reading. I handed out lollies to our little group in a circle on the floor while the teachers deliberately turned a blind eye. I put a finger to my lips to silence their delight but there was always one, usually Ben, Christopher or Nic, who couldn't control a snicker fit. I loved being in their classrooms but it was always hard to leave Christopher. He'd hug me tight around my waist and I'd bend down to kiss him.

'Don't go, Mama,' he sniffled in my ear.

'I'm just down the road, Cricket. What do you want me to make you for afternoon tea?'

'Pikelets,' he mumbled and reluctantly released me.

I reassured him I'd be waiting at the gate for him in a few hours 'with bells on'. I watched him through a secret window until he sat back down.

Ben and Nic were so much more self-assured. When I left their classrooms they'd wave goodbye from a distance and to make them laugh, I'd walk outside, jump up and down in front of the window like a jack-in-the-box then press my nose and lips to the glass to contort my face. I'm sure Ben was embarrassed but Nic would press his face to mine until the teacher made him return to his desk. I would still hear his laughter as I walked down the driveway.

In the afternoons, I'd wait for them at the gate and then we'd run home to make pikelets, smeared with apricot jam and piled high with whipped cream.

On the weekends, Phil and I took them all to Little Nippers, where they'd run in races along the beach and learn to swim in the pool. When they got older they'd learn life-saving in the ocean. Ben and Christopher were competitive but Nic preferred to make the adults laugh by deliberately falling over, ingesting a mouthful of sand, or somersaulting instead of running to the finish line. He always came last and didn't care. Ben usually came second to his much taller and stronger cousin Dan, but Christopher had to win and almost always did. When he lost, he berated himself. He wasn't a bad sport; he just needed to win to feel good about himself, a trait we tried to subdue with no success.

We eventually moved into a bigger house nearby in Bilgola where the boys, aged six, four and two, each had their own bedrooms. Christopher's room was next to Nic's and Ben's was across the hallway. Christopher hated the dark but pretended he didn't. At night, he wouldn't go upstairs unless Nic went with him. He'd say, 'Let's go upstairs, Nic, I wanna show you something', or 'I have a surprise for you'.

After a few nights Nic got tired of the fruitless rewards and refused to go with him. Christopher waited him out.

To solve the problem we appealed to Nic's humanity. Kind-hearted to his core, he made a game of going up the stairs to bed so Christopher would not feel ashamed. With Nic's approval, we moved his single bed into Christopher's room and pushed them together. The beds took up the entire space. We could barely close the door.

Three boys, so similar in looks, all blond and blue-eyed but so different in personality. Ben, the father figure, watchful, careful not to make mistakes. Christopher, the athlete, taking risks to perfect any given task. Nic, the intellect, wanting always to know why.

We were in a park one day when four-year-old Christopher climbed to the top of the jungle gym. Ben stood at the bottom, shaking his finger, telling him to get down because he might fall and hurt himself; Nic was sitting by the bench collecting and counting gum nuts.

Ben was serious, and sensible Christopher was a giggler who loved burping and farting. Nic was a practical joker who craved learning and making people laugh.

As brothers they were always close but as they grew older they found like-minded friends to satisfy their individual personalities and endeavours.

Ben found happiness on the water, sailing in a two-man dinghy, Christopher on the rugby field and Nic on stage.

Ben continued to keep a big-brother eye on Christopher when they were together and Nic just made everybody laugh. Phil and I enjoyed and watched over all of them. Phil coached Christopher's rugby team and I got involved with the school band of which all three were members. Ben, saxophone; Christopher, trumpet; and Nic, violin. That's what families did. Happy, normal families.

chapter 3

The ambulance doors closed with a whoosh. The engine came to life and Phil and I backed away as it turned to make its way out of the car park. I wondered whether it went back to base or straight to the morgue. I used to work at the morgue in Glebe. I covered the coroner's court for the Murdoch newspapers. I wrote stories about death and murder and one memorable case where a schizophrenic, who had discontinued his medication, cut off his landlady's head in front of her five-year-old daughter because he thought she was a witch. He baked her head in the oven. He was sentenced to 'Governor's Pleasure'—a sentence where prisoners are detained for an indefinite period for a serious offence. Their cases are reviewed based on a successful insanity defence. This is carried out by a reviewing body which must be satisfied that there has been a significant change in the defendant's attitude and behaviour. While serving his mandatory minimum period, the schizophrenic was forced to take his medication and was subsequently released. He was last seen pulling beers in rural New Zealand.

Christopher's friends drove to Mona Vale Hospital, assuming he was still alive. Phil and I trawled the car park looking for a tap.

The surf club was locked and in the dark we couldn't find a water source so we drove home. On the way Phil rang his parents and mine who called the rest of the family and close friends.

We unlocked the front door and while Phil threw his mouth under the kitchen tap, I checked on Nic.

The house was dark except for the red glow of the oven's digital clock. It said 1:38. It was so quiet we could hear the anguish in each other's shallow breathing. The lounge and kitchen suddenly lit up with an undulating glow as headlights came up and over the last bump of our driveway. People ran in, holding their chests, breathing heavily. Hands reached out to grope us. My parents were speechless. They had also lost a son; Jim died in a motorbike accident when he was twenty-three and Ben was just ten months old.

Someone handed me a scotch. I was worried Nic would wake up. Oh God, how was I going to tell Nic? How was I going to get Ben home safely? I felt sick. I wanted to go to bed. Phil walked in and out of each room like a ghost. I couldn't breathe. I was suffocating. I went outside. My ugg boots were covered in sand. Jack, who was still wet from the surf, came to sit with me. He was distraught.

'I'm sorry,' he said, covering his teary face with his big hands.

'It's not your fault,' I said, putting my arms around his shoulders.

We talked for a while but he was inconsolable and his parents took him home.

It was about 2:30 a.m. when the police arrived. They led Phil and me into the lounge room and sat opposite us. They looked sad and weary as though they had just lost a child. The policewoman who put the bag over my face to stop me hyperventilating sat quietly while the others asked the questions. I found out later this was her first night on the job.

'Was he on drugs?'

'I don't know.'

'Had he been drinking?'

'I don't know.'

'Was he at home with you tonight?'

'No. We were at Nic's play in North Sydney. Christopher had been at rugby training. I left some money for him to buy dinner. Jack said he had been at his house.'

'How did you know he was at the beach?'

'Jack called us. Just after 11:30.'

The room whitened as though a fine blanket of fog had seeped in under the closed doors. Faces blurred and voices muffled. Hands hovered over me and I wanted to scream. I heard my father ask the police to go.

'She's in shock,' he said.

Eventually everyone went home and I had another scotch then fell asleep fully dressed on the couch. Someone took off my ugg boots and covered me with a blanket. I woke up an hour later just as the sun peaked over the horizon, throwing light on the cliff where Christopher's friends had gathered to throw roses to the wind.

By eight o'clock the house had filled again. Someone handed me a cup of tea. The phone rang incessantly and our best friend Daisy, a big bear of a man, fielded the calls. I locked myself in my bedroom to ring Christopher and Nic's psychiatrist, Professor Gordon Parker. I needed his help—again. What would I say to Nic? His mental health was tenuous, he'd been diagnosed as suicidal, and I was petrified of losing another son. I blurted out what had happened the night before. Gordon was shocked. He asked to call me back and I could hear the distress in his voice. When he did a few minutes later, he went through what I should say to Nic methodically and kindly but I was terrified. I wanted to run a million miles away, for everyone to go home, to have yesterday back. Gordon came to our house later that day and talked to us all, especially Nic.

It would be hours before Nic awakened as the four different medications he swallowed each day, including an antipsychotic, antidepressant and a mood stabiliser, turned him into a zombie.

Phil rang Ben and asked him to come home because I had a bad migraine headache. Ben knew before he walked in the door—the driveway was choked with cars and friends and family milled about on the front deck. He sat next to me on the couch and put his head on my shoulder.

'What happened?'

I gave him broad details.

'Was it suicide?'

'We don't know yet. He may have slipped.'

'Why was he there?'

'I don't know.'

I crushed him to me as two tears splattered onto my arm. My heart stopped beating. I knew how it felt to lose a brother. I knew Ben and Nic would never get over Christopher's death. I knew their lives, like mine and Phil's, would never be the same again.

It was standing room only when Nic came down the stairs, wiping the sleep from his eyes.

'What's going on?' he said.

He looked at me, Phil and Ben then at the throng of friends and family. His mouth opened slightly as he screwed his eyes against the next moment of horror. I held onto him and hugged him hard. His body was rigid. Now he knew, too.

'It's Criddy!'

I nodded. He slumped onto the couch and I barricaded him with my arms. He cried and cried and cried. When his body finally stilled, Daisy, who is over six foot tall and big enough to play front-row forward, which he did for twenty-five years, took hold of Nic's hand and led him outside.

The boys have always loved Daisy. He's funny, kind and silly. He farts with a twenty-second practised restraint just to make them laugh. He rough-houses them but will also act as the father figure on the very rare occasion they think their father 'sucks'.

Flowers arrived, trays of sandwiches, cakes of every colour and flavour. Plates of food were shoved at me but I couldn't eat. The house was a maelstrom of activity and noise. It was deafening. I wandered in a daze from room to room, in and out, back and forth, looking for my family. Phil was teary—someone handed him a beer. Ben was politely talking to family and friends then disappeared upstairs to ring his girlfriend Sarah, who was volunteering in Vietnam. I was relieved to hear she was coming home the next day to be with Ben.

Nic was sitting on the edge of the fish pond, writing something on his forearm in black ink.

'Who's that?' I asked.

'You have to ring this number urgently.'

'Who is Brendan?'

'I don't know. He said he was from the eye hospital.'

'What does he want?'

'Just ring him, Mum. He says before eleven or it's too late.'

I looked at Daisy's watch which read 10:05. I couldn't be bothered but then Nic handed me the phone and ordered me to dial the number.

Brendan wanted Christopher's corneas. A blind sixteen-year-old girl from the country had travelled by train through the night in the hope we would agree to the donation.

When Christopher went for his driver's licence the year before, he asked me if he should tick the donor box.

'It's up to you.'

'Did you?'

'Yup.'

'I might as well. If I die I won't be needing them.'

As Christopher was under eighteen, I had to give my consent. Brendan said the young girl had been surgically prepped and there was a small window of time to operate. Apparently corneas were only viable within a twelve-hour period after death.

I wanted to say yes but I worried what Christopher would look like without his eyes. What if he needed them again—in heaven—somewhere. Hearing my thoughts, Brendan said they used prosthetic eyes and I wouldn't notice any difference. I said yes, handed the phone back to Daisy then vomited behind the bushes.

Somewhere in rural New South Wales, a young girl would see the world for the first time; the brilliant reds of a king parrot, the dusty yellows of wheat, even the black of night with its daggers of electric stars. I didn't know her name and she didn't know mine but she would have my son's eyes. His eyes were blue, metallic azure like the ocean before a storm.

Somewhere in a dusty country town or on a landscaped farm, a young girl would open her eyes to see the new day. She would gaze into the mirror and gasp at a beauty she never quite believed. She'd stroke her smooth skin and style her hair the way she always imagined. She'd marvel at the earth's colours, hug her mother and be able to see the love she'd only ever felt. She would dress herself in the shades she preferred, not what had been chosen for her. She now knew what purple looked like; and in time she would be able to see her son.

～

Lunchtime. A steady stream of friends and family filled our home. The funeral director arrived armed with paperwork and albums of photographs showing coffins of every size and shape. Thankfully, Phil's father Graham took over. Phil and I only had to choose a coffin; a wooden one with a gold cross because Christopher was religious. Phil's mother Moya chose the hymns and readings because she and Christopher shared that bond and Phil's brother Geoff, who owned a florist, ordered long-stemmed white roses. I wanted a cremation. I didn't want bugs gnawing at his flesh. We decided to have a service for family and close friends only at the crematorium.

The school wanted to hold a memorial service on the same day. A service sheet had to be made up. I asked Ben and Nic to take care of this, hoping to keep them busy.

The day was almost over. It had shuffled along in fitful, murky increments. People were still arriving while others left. I couldn't hug, talk, nod anymore. I had to be alone. Ben was in his room talking to Sarah on the phone and Nic had fallen asleep in a chair. I lifted him up and walked his sagging bulk to his room. He cried again as I tucked him under his doona. I held him and promised I would get him through this.

'Wake me up if you need me, Nic.'

He nodded, pulled Clowny to his neck then buried his face into his pillow.

If you had asked me, the day before Cricket died, what I feared most, I would have said losing Nic. He'd been in and out of institutions and several times he had admitted to me he wanted to die. Once, when he heard voices coming out of the radio ordering him to kill me, he locked himself in his room and forbade me to enter. He told me about it that night and then said, 'If something ever happens to me you'll have to sell this house.'

'Why?'

'Because you'd see me in every room and I know you couldn't live with that.'

Two months after Christopher died, Gordon admitted Nic into a psychiatric hospital. It was there, locked up in the acute wing, Nic sadly confessed that at 11:30 on the night Criddy died, he wanted to die too. We thought he was asleep but as Phil and I screamed out of the garage towards the headland, he had just hung up from Kids Helpline. At that exact same time, 11:30, Christopher's body was flying through the air.

chapter 4

It took more than an hour each morning for the boys to get from Bilgola to their school, Sydney Church of England Grammar School—or Shore, as it is known—in North Sydney, and the same for the return journey. When Nic started high school we decided to move to Balgowlah, a twenty-minute bus ride to school. We didn't have time to unpack and settle in before we knew Ben, who was sixteen, was in trouble. He was able to go to school but spent the rest of the time in his bedroom, coming out only to eat and shower. He was diagnosed with depression and it took several attempts to find the right medication.

During that same period thirteen-year-old Nic, who had been awarded music and academic scholarships, heard voices in his head; bad voices, mean and murderous. He wouldn't do his homework, was agitated and unable to concentrate. Phil and I were getting pressure from the school as he was not keeping up with the scholarship requirements.

Ben was in his room and Christopher was surfing with Murgy when on a warm November afternoon in 1999, Nic asked me to lie down next to him on his bed. He held my hand; his was clammy and trembling.

'What's up, Nic?'

'Something's wrong with me, Mum.'

'What do you mean?'

'I don't feel right—I don't feel like me. The walls are moving in. I see purple shapes in front of my eyes all the time and when I walk down the road, sometimes I want to kill people. I hear voices. Lots of them. They're in my head.'

I kissed him and reassured him we'd get help before stumbling out of the room. What was happening to my sons, my family? Ben was desperately unhappy, self-harming and locked away in his room. He didn't want to sail, see his friends or play music. His alto and tenor saxophones remained in their cases under his bed. So did Christopher's trumpet but only because it was not cool, as none of his rugby and surfing mates played instruments. Nic, who had shared the dux award the year before, couldn't even read a book. He tried to play his violin but the sweep of his bow was discordant and grating, even to his confused ears.

I didn't understand his confession. Was it his creative and overactive imagination or a verbalisation of some dreamlike state? Was it real? And if so, how did the voices get inside his brain? It frightened Phil and me. We knew about depression and OCD, obsessive compulsive disorder, but nothing about psychosis. This was something we couldn't deal with on our own.

Phil's sister Jane recommended Bill, a psychologist who lived next door to her. Over several months he tried to help Nic but couldn't diagnose him. Bill recommended that Nic see a psychiatrist who could diagnose and medicate him. One was recommended and we were able to get an appointment the following week.

We were given an extended session of thirty minutes on our first visit. The others, the psychiatrist told us, would be fifteen minutes in duration. I wondered how anyone could possibly work out the mind's demons in such short increments. After spending twenty minutes establishing he had a higher IQ than Nic, the psychiatrist, with a smug delighted air, diagnosed OCD and medicated him accordingly. Nic dramatically deteriorated with each fifteen-minute session. He refused to go to school, spending most of the day in bed.

Without admitting he could be wrong, the psychiatrist suggested we send Nic to Rivendell, an historic child and adolescent mental health facility in the Sydney suburb of Concord on the Parramatta River. Rivendell is a twenty-bed inpatient and outpatient hospital. Its founding director was Professor Marie Bashir, a revered psychiatrist and later governor of New South Wales. Down the road the 2000 Sydney Olympics had just begun. While we waited for a consultation and possible acceptance into Rivendell, another psychologist, Adam, was recommended by Nic's school counsellor.

At the same time, Phil and I finally admitted to each other that we hated living in Balgowlah. I secretly called it the madhouse, blaming it for the destruction of our happy family unit. We'd only lived there for six months but I couldn't wait to pack up and move. Phil found a house in Avalon with hundred-year-old cabbage palms and a shed for the chooks. It was only a kilometre from the beach. On the night we moved in, Adam called me after his weekly session with Nic.

'Nic needs urgent help,' he said. 'He's suicidal. He has to see a psychiatrist immediately.'

Phil and I panicked. I spoke to Elizabeth, a psychiatrist at Rivendell the next morning. She could hear my fear and hysteria and said I could bring him in the following day.

I sat by Nic's bed throughout the night without sleep. I watched and wept as his body twitched and I held my ears as the voices made him scream out deranged gobbledegook into the dark.

As the sun rose, I quickly showered while Phil kept watch over Nic. We told Ben and Christopher that Nic was seeing a new doctor. They had no idea then how sick he was. We dropped them at the bus stop and were on the road with Nic by seven.

Nic was assessed in the morning and by early afternoon he was given a place at Rivendell. I hoped he would stay as an inpatient so he would receive around-the-clock care but he said he'd be lonely without us. After several months, Elizabeth, unable to definitively diagnose him, asked for Nic to see another Rivendell psychiatrist for a second opinion. After another month he, too, was unsure but diagnosed Nic as having a prodrome, or psychosis risk syndrome, an early symptom or set of symptoms that might indicate the start of a disease, in Nic's case, schizophrenia or bipolar disorder.

There was a school located in the grounds of Rivendell and once patients were established they were expected to attend classes. Nic struggled with the Year 7 math curriculum. He pretended he was proud of himself when he solved a simple equation but we saw his veiled disillusion and I tried not to cry or rip up the fucking grid paper.

Nic made some friends at Rivendell, even though they were mostly inpatients. One had a deep and musical tenor voice, another would one day work for a major confectionary company; and then there was Simon. He loved rocks. Every day when I picked up Nic, Simon would run to me with a 'special' rock he'd found in the large grounds of Rivendell. The next day when he asked me what I did with it, I told him I was building a frog pond. I ended up with more than a hundred rocks. We filled the pond with water and when we heard the first croak, we named the pond after Simon. He was delighted when we told him.

One day Christopher came with me to pick up Nic and as I talked to the doctor, my sons wandered off to the riverbank and sat together on a rock. Their heads were together in deep conversation. When we arrived home, Christopher whispered to me that he had the same illness as Nic.

Shocked and scared, I asked him, 'Why do you think that?'

'Everything he is feeling, I'm feeling too. Everything.'

The next day I asked Nic's psychiatrist to see Christopher and after several sessions she diagnosed severe anxiety and depression. He, too, was medicated.

〜

Three sons—all of them inflicted with mental illness. I didn't know how Phil and I were going to cope. Everything we ever hoped for our children had ended. I knew Nic's dream of becoming a vet was over. I knew he wouldn't even finish high school. I knew Christopher would hide his illness from his friends and the strain of that would cripple him. And Ben, who had survived his shorter fight with depressive illness, would stand quietly by, powerless as he witnessed the mental disintegration of the brothers he always protected. Phil and I would love and protect them but our marriage would be under constant strain as we had no time for each other. We would silently blame each other. Too tough, too weak, bad genes. My mother and Phil's brother had depression, I had had postpartum depression and there was OCD on both sides. What chance did they have?

Christopher became increasingly wary of Nic's moods. One moment Nic was raging, speaking fast and not sleeping, and the next we were unable to get him out of bed. Due to the cocktail of drugs, Nic would go from a thin 50 kilos to more than 100 kilos in just over a year, and his mental state was deteriorating daily. He wrote in his diary that he had to clear his 'unclean mind' by ritualistic killing. He was too young to understand what that meant.

'I'll spare you the details of my sick thoughts,' he wrote. 'It's not something you want to hear or I want to tell you but the thing I do in my head to make up for it is a murder.

'I have two of those corn cutting things the Grim Reaper uses and basically I slash some unknown guy to pieces. It is violent, frequent and very, very symmetrical. One slash from each weapon from the sides to the middle and through. Step one is then done again. This wipes the slate clean but doesn't always get rid of the thought. Sometimes I have to keep on doing it harder and faster until it goes away. When the bad thought is about a family member, I have to do the ritual with more power.'

This is what madness looked like. This was how Nic saw his small world, this was what he woke to each day. This was why he, too, would want to die.

The purple dots swimming constantly in his vision were geometric, which he said made him able to see into the future, one in which he feared he had no place. He told me reality wasn't real and that his waking hours were like a dream. Movies, television, video games and other stimuli became real to him.

'There are two of me,' he said as we sat on the couch together one night during this time. 'I don't mind sitting with myself because one of me entertains the other me. But sometimes one of me scares me. I don't know what's on the outside or what's on the inside of me anymore. I am confused about who I am. My mind frightens me.'

Then he told me he didn't want to live anymore but he felt stuck because it would be unfair to his family and that I'd never get over his loss.

～

Christopher no longer wanted to be at home and used any excuse to leave. He begged us to allow him to board at school. We knew he was becoming increasingly distressed watching his suicidal brother sink into the depths of madness. He was frightened for him and because he was sick himself, he knew he couldn't help Nic.

Christopher continued to surf, play rugby and socialise with his mates and girlfriend Annabel; only Ally and Jack, the two friends with him at the headland that night, knew he had depression, but even they were unaware of the serious extent of it.

He started to binge-drink and smoke marijuana. We begged him not to, as research was starting to show that dope made depression worse and increased suicide ideation in adolescents. But he ignored us, taking more and more risks with his life. We found out after the funeral that he had crashed his car while drunk several times. He was self-medicating and, like so many other seventeen-year-olds, believed he was bulletproof. The slide from a happy and healthy teenager into the dark hole was swift and covert, mentally and physically.

Playing for his school's First Fifteen rugby team had always been Christopher's dream. If he had a bad game and was dropped to the Seconds, it devastated him. Phil and I knew it was the one area in his life which made him feel confident. When the team was first selected, he wasn't chosen. The following season he made it, playing half-back then breakaway. Several weeks into the season he became ill with ear and throat infections and had to have his tonsils removed. A few weeks after that he had to have a lower leg operation to lengthen the muscles which weren't growing at the same rate as his bones, causing excruciating pain when he walked or ran. Then, several months later, the other leg had to be operated on. He was told to exercise both legs constantly to stretch the muscles but then he contracted glandular fever and was bedridden for several months. Since he was unable to exercise, the operations were a waste of time. When he finally recovered, he fought to get back into the team and when he finally did, he played in constant pain. He took painkillers and anti-inflammatories just to get through a match.

The autopsy found both of these substances in his system. I think he knew he only had a few games left to play because of his injuries. He didn't tell us this. He didn't tell us anything and we were so frightened of losing Nic we didn't realise how seriously troubled Christopher was.

While he was boarding, he was caught smoking dope, an instantly expellable offence. The school's hierarchy met to discuss what to do with Christopher, and Phil and I waited by the phone for hours. Eventually the deputy principal, Graham Robertson, rang to say that due to our family's circumstances, the school had decided to give Christopher another chance. He was 'gated' which meant he was not allowed out on weekends.

Several weeks later he was caught smoking cigarettes. After a distressed call from Christopher, the headmaster Bob Grant called Phil to attend an urgent meeting with him, Graham Robertson, Reverend Matthew Pickering and Antony Weiss, the House Master. I stayed at home with Nic.

Phil reported back that Bob was well aware of our problems with Nic and the effect his illness had on Christopher and our family. The meeting allowed everyone to offer their perspective on what punishment should be allocated. It was very apparent to Phil how much these men liked and cared for our son. Phil said they each took turns to speak, pitching hard, attesting to Crick's good nature and character.

After about half an hour, Bob sighed deeply then said: 'This requires the wisdom of Solomon.' He asked them all to leave the room while he deliberated. They went back to Antony's lounge room where Christopher was waiting.

'I knew that Crick had backed Bob into a corner,' Phil told me later.

Headmaster Bob Grant had already made a brave decision to allow Christopher to stay at school. We feared that if he was expelled it would be a disaster for him as, ironically, he needed the structure and discipline the school offered. It would also mean he wouldn't be able to play rugby and that would devastate him. 'I believed Bob had no choice,' Phil said. 'Teachers, students and parents expected direct action.'

During his deliberation, Bob called Professor Gordon Parker—a leading psychiatrist in mental health, his friend and a former student at Shore—to ask him to see Christopher, which he did at ten the following morning. At the time Phil said to me that asking Gordon to see Crick showed Bob's immense wisdom and compassion.

Professor Parker diagnosed severe depression and anxiety. Bob allowed Christopher to stay at school but on Gordon's recommendation he was to live at home and attend as a day student. The school was now aware of his illness and, just as it did for Nic, went about providing the support and understanding necessary to help him through the days and weeks ahead.

But Christopher wasn't coping. He stopped attending classes, spending the day in a friend's boarding room. After several weeks it was decided he had to leave school altogether. Headmaster Grant allowed him to continue playing rugby in the hope that connection to school would encourage him to want to return.

He never did. He had nothing to fill in his days. For six months he lived with Ally in a cottage at the back of her mother's house and, while she went to school, he lay in bed watching movies. Phil and I begged him to come home but except for quick visits, we hardly ever saw him. When we asked him why he couldn't live with us, he said he was lonely at home. That was the beginning of the fast descent; we just didn't realise it then. Despite many warning signs which were frightening in hindsight, I didn't think for a second he was suicidal. I had taken my eye off the ball.

～

On the night after the funeral I was sitting alone and in the dark by our pond in Avalon trying to get away from the crowds inside our home. The sliding door suddenly opened and two women, I couldn't see who they were, sat down on the white stone bench near where I was hiding. They both lit up a cigarette, the glow two full-stops in the midnight sky. This was the same bench I had found Christopher sitting on a few months earlier at four in the morning. Phil and I had gone to bed early and at some point I heard his car come up the driveway and went back to sleep. Just before four I woke to check on him. His bed was empty. I searched the house and, unable to find him, frantically woke Phil. He, too, looked everywhere. We called his name, opened and shut every door. Then we circled the outside perimeter, finding him in the dark on the stone bench by the pond. He was agitated and high on some drug. He had his head in his hands, dazed and disorientated, and his body was shaking. I'd never seen him like this before.

'What have you taken, Cricket?' I yelled.

'Nothing.'

'You have. You can hardly talk.'

'One.'

'One what?'

'Ritalin.'

Ritalin is a stimulant drug given mostly for ADHD, attention deficit hyperactive disorder.

'Where did you get it from? Phil asked.

'My friend's little brother.'

We lugged him to bed.

At eight in the morning I called Gordon. He knew by Christopher's described physical and emotional state that he had taken more than one Ritalin. Christopher finally admitted he took nine. Gordon told me to bring him in urgently. The dose, he said, could have been fatal. He talked to him privately and then organised for Christopher to see him and a clinical psychologist weekly. It was her notes and Christopher's responses to her questions I would find in his rugby bag two weeks after his death.

That night I waited for the women to finish their cigarettes so I could escape from my hiding place.

'She's going to blame herself,' one of them said.

'Yeah, I probably would too,' the other agreed. 'I'd feel like a failure—being a mother—you know?'

'Yup, with drugs and alcohol these days, it's very hard. If you can get them to eighteen ...'

Eighteen. That parental, magical, safe number. Many times I had said to Phil that if we could just get all our sons to eighteen I knew they would survive. Christopher died seven weeks before his eighteenth birthday, and one day before the start of spring.

chapter 5

I hated baking. Having seen my early attempts at wowing my children with special homemade cakes, my friend Deby, with the best intentions, bought me the *Women's Weekly Birthday Cake* recipe book.

'How can you stuff up a number one?' she guffawed when I set Nic's first cake on the dining table.

She laughed even harder when Ben's number four, laced with chocolate icing and smarties, was backwards. When I thumbed through the book looking for an easy recipe for Ben's fifth birthday, I settled on a castle. I was glad we didn't have girls. Who but a professional baker could possibly make a doll or an open-lidded jewellery box?

The castle looked easy enough—two squares on top of each other and upside-down ice-cream cones for the turrets at each corner. White icing—no problem. I even stuck some red paper on toothpicks for the corner flags, which wasn't in the picture. All was going to plan. The boys were fighting over who would lick the knife and I told them to wait till I'd finished. I could tell they were impressed as I slopped the first mound of icing into the centre. I delicately smoothed it over the surface then up the sides of the cones. Each boy was entrusted with inserting a flag, their hands hovering over the cones anxiously. Suddenly all the cones fell over under the weight of the icing which, I discovered, was too thick. We resurrected them sans icing and tried with another batch. This time the icing was too thin and dribbled down the corrugated curves in unappetising lumps.

'It doesn't matter, Mama,' Ben said. 'It'll still taste good.'

And it didn't matter, as halfway through the party Ben cut his head open on the corner of the wall while riding on the shoulders of an older boy. We spent most of his birthday in the doctor's surgery.

The boys loved their birthdays. They got to choose their favourite meal to eat at home or we'd take them out to a restaurant. We each bought a present for the birthday boy and I'd tie a balloon in a loop at the back of their pants or shorts. The birthday cake was the grand finale and there would be several more disasters before they each opted for a bought cake.

Christopher asked for a football when he turned eight. It would be his last homemade birthday cake. He invited his friends to the local football oval and we played games until they became bored and set up their own teams. When it was time for cake, candles and happy birthday, the teams gathered around while I took out the cake from the esky. Silence. Then laughter, the loudest from Deby who declared, 'It looks like a turd.'

The boys and two girls giggled at Deby's irreverence—I was devastated.

'It does look like a football,' Christopher said, wrapping his dirty arm around my waist.

I was happy to cut it up and pass it out.

chapter 6

I don't remember the last time I saw Christopher. Maybe it was on the Saturday before, at his rugby match, but it could have been Sunday. I just don't remember anymore. He had given up on his family, his school and many of his close friends. He lived with Ally and although he came home occasionally to say hello or to pick up some clothes, he was always anxious to leave.

He moved slowly through his days looking for something to do. His only commitments were his twice-weekly training sessions and the game on Saturday. He didn't want to come home because there was tension there. Phil and I were scared—frightened of Nic's illness, petrified we were going to lose him. We huddled around Nic, shadowed him, checked on him constantly. He had also left school, forfeiting his scholarships.

On Tuesday, two nights before Christopher died, I called him just to hear his voice and to find out about his appointment with Gordon. The next day he was to see his clinical psychologist. Both would tell me later they had asked Christopher if he was suicidal. He assured them he wasn't.

He was out to dinner at Avalon's local Thai with his 'adopted' family when I called. He seemed happy and was talkative for a change. I was jealous he was able to fit in with someone else's family, be close to someone else's mother. I knew he'd been drinking.

'When you come home be careful of the blind possum,' I told him.

Every night 'our' possum would crawl up the driveway, banging into the concrete walls before finding the spot by the fountain where we scattered quartered apples and bananas, one day past pleasant eating.

'Is he still alive?' Christopher asked, not having seen him for a few weeks.

'Yes. He's at the top of the driveway. Don't run over him.'

'You're funny, Mum. You know he's going to die. Something will get him.'

'I know but I don't want it to be you.'

I knew he'd stay at Ally's and wouldn't come home that night but I hoped he heard the longing in my voice. I wanted him home so badly. I needed the normalcy of my family of five again but mostly I wanted to watch him, though his daily absences did give me respite from the constant tension of negative parenting. Don't do that, don't go there, get off the phone, walk the dog, don't drink, don't smoke, don't, don't, don't. I felt guilty I couldn't love him in the way he needed and I was hurt that he didn't seem to need my love.

Phil was gentle with Christopher, encouraging him towards good behaviour. I was angry he was adding to the family stress. While Nic lay about, drugged and miserable, Christopher was partying, drinking and smoking dope. I didn't realise then that he was self-medicating.

I lived in fear for Nic and the phone call from police or a friend that Christopher had wrapped his car around a telegraph pole. I'd had calls before. Once, when Christopher was twelve, he was staying at a friend's house when they met up with two older boys in the grounds of a primary school on a Sunday. The police arrested the two sixteen-year-olds for breaking into the canteen and although the two younger boys were innocent, the call was intended as a warning. Christopher was full of remorse.

Then, when he was fourteen, he disappeared on Halloween night. He was staying at Jack's house but a call from his mother in the early hours, asking if the boys were with us, sent us all into panic. I called the local police to tell them our sons were missing.

'So is everyone else's son on this night,' the bored constable said.

'But he's never done this before,' I retaliated.

'That's what they all say. If he's not home after twenty-four hours, and I'm sure he will be, you can contact us again.'

Phil and I drove around Avalon and its surrounding suburbs for hours. We eventually found them at the home of their friend Erica. They had got into a fight with a group from the western suburbs which had it in for the 'beach boys'. Erica's mother was woken and while they told tales of their conquest, she looked over Christopher's injured hand, confirmed it wasn't broken or sprained then bandaged his raw bleeding knuckles.

'I'm sorry I didn't call,' Christopher said when I grounded him for a week.

'He's such a gorgeous boy,' Erica's mother said. 'He was just protecting his mates.'

That's how Cricket got away with everything. All he had to do was smile, say sorry, promise not to repeat his misdemeanour. Everyone loved him, except for a few of his school teachers who couldn't see or didn't care to pander to his vulnerability. Those who loved him did and tried to nurture him. His personality was infectious. He was loving, protective, loyal and generally honest. He was his group's leader but few saw the fear he kept corked—except for one night, and that was excused by his friends as too much alcohol.

He had just turned sixteen. He and his mates were at our house for a barbecue. Phil and I had gone out to dinner. When we arrived home, one of his friends intercepted us at the door to tell us Christopher was upset. We raced out to him.

He stumbled towards me and threw his long arms around me and slumped to put his head on my shoulder. He was sobbing.

'I'm sorry, Mum, I'm sorry,' he said over and over again.

I led him inside and tried to seat him but he wouldn't let me go.

'What's wrong, Cricket?'

'I'm sorry, I'm sorry.'

'What for?'

'I'm scared.'

Two friends walked in and heaved his arms around their shoulders and carried him to the lounge room where I had covered the floor with mattresses so they could all stay the night.

In the morning he told us he'd had too much to drink and wasn't really scared.

'You've got to stop drinking, Cricket.'

'Yeah, I know. I will.'

He kissed me on the cheek before grabbing his surfboard to catch the high tide.

~

We were at home when he called us from his boarding room the following year.

'Mum! I've done something really bad.'

My heart stopped and I took a deep breath.

'What, Cricket?'

'I'm really sorry, Mum.'

'What have you done? It's okay, you can tell me.'

That's when he confessed he'd been caught smoking dope, then a few weeks later, cigarettes. That's when we first met Professor Parker.

Gordon Parker is a distinguished, humble and quietly spoken man. He is Professor of Psychiatry at the University of New South Wales and the founder of the Black Dog Institute. He has written several books including—with co-author Kerrie Eyers—*Navigating Teenage Depression* and *Tackling Depression at Work*. He exudes a caring warmth which put us all at ease on our first appointment. He spoke to Christopher privately first, then invited Phil and me into his office to share his plan to help our son. I trusted him instantly and was relieved he would try to get Christopher back on track. At the time Nic was floundering at Rivendell as psychiatrists there struggled to diagnose him. On our second visit with Christopher to Gordon, I summoned the courage to ask if he'd see Nic. He didn't hesitate.

Both Christopher and Nic deeply admired and respected Gordon. We never had to struggle to get them to keep their appointments.

'He's a good guy,' Christopher said after the initial appointment and we knew, from him, that was high praise.

In a few short weeks Nic became reliant on Gordon, not making a move without speaking to him first. Gordon was and still is Nic's hero and mentor.

chapter 7

~~

It was the last day of spring, Saturday, August 31st, 2002. Christopher had been dead for thirty-six hours. If he was still alive, he'd be driving to North Sydney with Jack to the oval where Shore's First Fifteen would take on Newington in the season's penultimate battle. Christopher's team-mates had decided the day before that they could not play. They all said they couldn't go on the field without their mate. After several meetings Jack tearfully suggested that Cricket would have wanted them to play. The team reluctantly agreed. A 500-strong guard of honour stretched across the entire field and Ben and Nic were asked to lead the players through the pitched tunnel of arms. Wearing black armbands, the team bowed their heads in a minute's silence, as did every private school team that day at three o'clock. Phil and I sat on the deck at home with a handful of friends and received regular updates.

Murgy had just finished his match in the Second Fifteen and was sitting under a tree at the oval. He was distraught and being comforted by some friends when he was asked to fill in for an injured player in the Firsts. He didn't want to, but—thirty minutes into the game with Shore behind seven points to nil—forced himself onto the field. At halftime, the players gathered in a circle and were told by Captain Danny Clark that they all had to lift, had to fight, had to win for Chris. The scores were deadlocked with five minutes left on the clock. Suddenly, the ball was passed with speed and accuracy to Jack who took off in a sprint like never before and scored under the posts. Shore won 20–13.

Rugby was crucial to Christopher. Playing in the top team for his school and being with his close mates gave him a high which blanketed his depression and anxiety—at least while he was playing or training.

When he was a young boy he would sleep in his rugby guernsey with his rugby ball under one arm, Bunny under the other. On Sunday mornings, Phil would take him down for kicking practice and during the week I'd throw him passes in the driveway.

It was this same rugby ball along with his boots which Phil put into his coffin. One of his team-mates, also named Chris, asked us to put in the much-cherished socks he had worn when he was selected for the prestigious Sydney Schoolboys team.

Nic put a *Playboy* magazine by his feet; Ben, a can of beer near his right hand. I wanted to put Bunny near his head but Phil said I'd regret it so I put in a condom instead. Bunny is now in my bedroom on top of a chest filled with all that I have left of Christopher, including the videos we filmed on a hired camera when the boys were very young.

∼

Christopher loved making people laugh. One of the videos was shot in our tiny bathroom. The boys, aged five, four and two, were all undressing and laughing. The bath was filling high with bubbles. Ben and Nic carefully lowered their bodies into the warm water followed by Christopher who jumped from a height, sending clouds of bubbles into the air. He covered his face with them and ho-hoed like Santa. Ben told him to be careful and Nic giggled, which spurred him on to stand up and launch into his favourite jingle while providing the inglorious hand movements: 'Wash your penis, wash your penis.'

He loved toilet humour, too. One night when we were singing our Street Light Man song, I pointed out the moon which was peaking over the neighbour's roof in the eastern sky. It was a waning gibbous moon, a plump crescent I named Banana Man. I told them to imagine it had eyes, a nose and a smiley mouth.

'Now pretend to draw on him,' I said.

Ben gave him glasses and Nic gave him a red and white striped cap, which he said looked like the one worn by Dr Seuss's *Cat in the Hat*. Christopher gave him a 'a big, fat bogey' which he said was green and hanging like glue out of his nose. He folded in two, laughing uncontrollably.

When he was sixteen he asked Phil and me if it was possible to get a sexually transmitted disease from a 'blow job'. We smiled and asked him if he'd had one. He rolled his eyes as if to say, 'Hasn't everyone?' A few days later he drove up the driveway and stopped the car near where I was weeding. He dropped his pants and said: 'See, you can. Look at all these red spots on my dick.'

I ordered him to make an appointment with our family doctor, John Eccles.

This is what I loved about him; his naivety, his openness and honesty. We could talk about anything; no subject was taboo for me, though not always for Phil, who was far more conservative and sensible. I always insisted on having dinner together around our round dining table and would encourage the boys to talk about the greater questions of life. One night we opened a discussion about homosexuality. I said there was nothing wrong with it and if they ever felt they were different sexually they must be open with us and we'd help them navigate through what could be a difficult existence (this was the early 1990s). After ten minutes of discussion, Phil, who had been silent throughout, suddenly chimed in with, 'Or you could do yourself a favour and not be gay.'

We all laughed; I was the only one who knew Phil was deadly serious.

~

We were all so happy then. The boys were growing strong and seemed contented and confident. We were so proud of them, not so much for their achievements or because they were smart—but for their kindness and sensitivity to others. When they were all at Shore, one teacher said to me: 'What an asset the Newling boys are to this school.'

Ben loved music and started up Shore's summer sailing school and Christopher was in the top rugby teams and won the religion award one year. Nic, on scholarship, won many public-speaking awards and his debating team was considered one of the best.

But then, at thirteen, a battlefield of combatants fought for the rights to Nic's mind and a frightened young boy surrendered. At fifteen, when all medication was failing to help, Gordon suggested ECT, electroconvulsive therapy, which he said had promising results for some drug-resistant patients. ECT is a psychiatric treatment in which seizures are electrically induced in anaesthetised patients for therapeutic effect. It can often 'reset' electrical and chemical circuits that are presumed to be disrupted in those with psychotic and melancholic depression and who have not responded to orthodox antidepressant medications.

I was upset and nervous when I took Nic to the Prince of Wales Hospital in Randwick on a cold Monday morning for the first of possibly six electric shock treatments. I stayed with him while they prepared him in theatre. They asked me to leave before they anaesthetised him and attached the electrodes to his head. He smiled at me bravely as I kissed him on the cheek.

'Don't worry, Mum. It's not going to hurt. Go have a coffee.'

I walked through the thick plastic flaps, down the long corridor and, feeling faint, leant against the wall until my breathing slowed. I didn't realise I was crying until a nurse offered me a box of tissues and settled me into a nearby chair.

All I could see was the image of Jack Nicholson strapped to a bed against his will in *One Flew Over the Cuckoo's Nest* and I felt guilty for agreeing to allow my son's brain to be zapped. My mobile phone rang.

I thanked the nurse and stumbled to the entrance. It was Dr Eccles with Christopher's 'red spots on dick' results. Christopher had chlamydia, a very infectious sexually transmitted disease. Dr Eccles stressed that Christopher must inform his girlfriend urgently as it was particularly harmful to women. I wondered if there was more than one girl.

After a few hours Nic was allowed to go home. He would be back in two days for the second treatment. When Christopher came in from school I told him about Dr Eccles's phone call and to let his girlfriend Annabel know, and anyone else who may be an 'interested party'. He rolled his eyes and smiled, giving me a little pat on my back. Then he rubbed Nic's head and asked him if the zapping hurt. Nic stuck his tongue out and let it loll. He dropped his head, forcing two drops of dribble to roll down his T-shirt. He looked up at his brother, crossed his eyes, threw his head back then jerked his body into a frenzy. When the performance ended Christopher grabbed him around the neck and, laughing hysterically, they made their way upstairs.

I laughed with them, too, then out of sight I cried silently into my teatowel.

chapter 8

The blind possum died two days after Christopher. The mound of bananas and apples was left uneaten. Shadow, our golden retriever, wouldn't eat either. She was sick with grief for Christopher, vomiting every meal. She was so sad she whimpered for most of each day while she lay at my feet with her head on her paws and she became distressed if left alone. She, too, would die a year later from cancer. Lisa, our cat, frightened by the crowds, disappeared for two days.

Christopher loved all animals. He was eight years old when he asked to go to Waratah Park, a famous Sydney wildlife park and home to TV's Skippy the Bush Kangaroo, on one of our 'kidnap' days. Each year I would secretly arrange with their teachers to take them out of class for a day. I'd whisper in their ears that I was kidnapping them. Their eyes would open wide and they'd hurry to pack up their little satchels. We'd hold hands as we ran down the driveway into my waiting car. They got to choose where they wanted to go.

Christopher loved Waratah Park. He especially wanted to see the wombats, his favourite animal. We darted around the bush tracks, laughing, exploring and feeding the animals. Then we sat on the park bench to eat our peanut butter sandwiches.

When we got home that day Christopher asked for an animal of his own.

Shadow was Ben's dog and Nic had a cage full of mice in every stage of development. Lisa belonged to the whole family. Christopher wanted a rabbit which he would name Lawnmower. Often he'd take his stuffed bunny to his real bunny so Lawnmower wouldn't feel lonely.

I wanted to bury the blind possum but I couldn't find its body. I didn't believe in souls and reincarnation but Christopher did, and somehow it was important that the animal's decrepit little body was safe in the warm earth, away from predators.

Christopher found solace in the spiritual world and believed in the afterlife. He loved the Buddha he kept on his bedside table and surrounded it with moonstones and incense.

The day before we had to view Christopher's body I snuck into his bedroom and locked the door behind me. I had to find something to place in his coffin. His room felt warm and airy in contrast to the heavy, claustrophobic cloak which had fallen over the rest of the house.

Loss, the dead weight of it, had enfolded our lives, our grief making us strangers to each other and the outside world. Silence filled the empty rooms as we all crouched in darkened corners looking for something to do, something to say. We could feel each other's misery as we watched, through suspicious eyes, our former selves fail at simulating life as we knew it a few days past.

My first instinct was to pack everything in boxes so I'd never have to look at them again. If the reminders were gone, I would not have to grieve as hard or for as long. Then I remembered what a friend had told me a few years earlier about the death of her niece. Her sister had not touched her daughter's room since her death twenty years ago. Each night she would light a candle, pray by her bed and often sleep in it, curled in a foetal position clinging to her daughter's doll. It was a shrine no one was allowed to enter. Nothing had blunted her grief and when I first heard the story I thought it was because of her shrine, but then as I stood in Christopher's five-day-old lifeless room, it hit me. Nothing mattered now. It was over.

I could do whatever I wanted because nothing would mollify my grief.

I picked up the diary which was next to his daily pack of inspirational cards on his desk, opened on page 241, August 29th, 2002.

There was also a book filled with his rugby training notes and long-forgotten school assignments. I scrutinised all the notes looking for clues. His school diary revealed his unhappiness and uncertainty, his apathy and despair. His personal diary began on October 15th, 2001, and ended the next year on February 15th. The first thing he wrote was: 'Why am I off track: no goals, no certain future, no track to follow.' After that, the pages were blank. Perhaps after that, he had already decided life would soon be over. The four months of notes showed his fight to find some sense in his troubled thoughts, to change the negatives, to find the will to live. Each week ended with a famous quote.

Tumbled together in his top drawer were a box of condoms, letters from girlfriends, his boyhood Matchbox cars, a candle and a book I gave him when he was five—*I'll Always Love You* by Hans Wilheim. It's a story about Elfie, 'The World's Best Dog'. The boy and Elfie grew up together and when Elfie was naughty and she was scolded, the family didn't tell her that they loved her anyway. They thought she just knew. As the boy got taller, Elfie got older and bigger. The boy carried her upstairs to his room each night and laid her on a soft pillow. Before they went to sleep he would say to her, 'I'll always love you.' He knew she understood. Soon after, Elfie died during the night. The boy's brother and sister loved Elfie a lot and were sad but they had never told her they loved her. The boy was very sad, too, but it helped to remember that he had told her he loved her every night.

On the inside cover I had written: 'To my beautiful Cricket. I'll always love you—Mama.' Next to it was a tiny lock of Christopher's hair under a yellowing piece of sticky tape.

I know I told him I loved him but maybe as he got older, not enough. I was angry and yelled at him a lot. *Don't go! Do this! Go! Come! Stop! Stop!* I yelled at him when Ally, the girl he was living with, dyed his hair black. I was angry when he talked on the phone till the early hours of the morning, leaving his unfinished homework in a pile on his desk. I was upset that many of his depressed, heartbroken or unhappy girlfriends asked him for his counsel when he was desperately sad himself. They didn't know he needed help and he never asked for it. We fought for days over his insistence to have an eyebrow ring and when Ben's girlfriend Sarah reluctantly told us she had seen him swigging beer while driving, he denied it and I got angry because he had lied. I was most angry that he made us worry about him when we had so much stress with Nic.

Christopher's tattered blue bunny had fallen between his two pillows. Its fur was matted, the stuffing leaking out from the back of its flattened head. One cheek was threadbare from too much loving and the tag which little Christopher used to rub around his ear and nose while sucking his thumb had long gone. I lay down next to it and held it tightly to me. I wondered how many tears Bunny had absorbed over the years.

What would become of Bunny; who would love it now?

I lay on Christopher's bed, hugged his pillow to me and inhaled the lingering traces of him. Tomorrow, I promised myself, I'd wash his sheets, pack up his things then close the door. I told myself I must never go back in. I didn't for a few days, but when no one was at home I'd go in just to be with him, to smell him. I slid between his sheets and willed the world to stop. I knew, in time, this room would send me mad; this empty, deathly, soundless crypt, the black and cream striped curtains he chose, pulled together tight to block out life.

In time there would be nothing left to see, touch, smell or hear. Diseased senses, hidden fears, putrescent moments and useless monuments collected over a short life, all crushed and shrivelled into plastic boxes—keepsakes for the children he would never have.

I scoured over each item, every piece of paper, hoping for a clue as to why he needed to die. Was there a hidden meaning in a letter from a friend who begged him to leave his girlfriend for her? Another pleaded with him to bear his soul, to trust her with his problems. Was there a sign in the memorial card from the funeral of a mate who threw himself off a bridge four months earlier?

His rugby bag, found in the boot of his car at the headland, was by his bed. In one pocket was a crinkled tube of Dencorub, his mouthguard, anti-inflammatory pills and an anti-anxiety drug. In another, Panadeine, bandages and a water bottle. In the bag itself were his headgear, boots and tracksuit. Hidden underneath were the notes from his session with the psychologist the day before he died.

Seeing his small, neat and masculine handwriting shocked me. But it was what he wrote that devastated me when I realised how sad and confused he really was, how quickly he had plummeted into dark despair. He was lonely and frightened and he couldn't reach out to anyone. He had visited a friend, Emma, the night before, on August 28th. Her parents had asked him to stay for dinner but he said he had to get home. It was Emma he was talking to as he stood on the headland's precipice the following night. Emma heard the phone go dead as it smashed on the rocks below. She would tell me much later that when she last saw him, he had hugged her tightly and it felt to her like a goodbye.

On August 29th he rang another close friend, Lara, to ask if he could come over to watch *The Footy Show* with her, a Thursday ritual they often enjoyed together, but she had to work.

On August 27th he and Ally were lying in bed watching *Pulp Fiction*. He wrote about the movie on the back of a Cognitive Distortions Test that I found in his rugby bag.

'All the conversations are pointless,' he wrote. 'Why do they do that? It is depressing that people talk about completely uninteresting things just to avoid an uncomfortable silence. It seems like they're only interested in superficial and petty topics.'

When asked to describe his fears about being away from home and living with a sixteen-year-old girl, he wrote: 'I was lying down next to her and started getting really agitated. I couldn't get myself to feel anything but disgust and I had a sick feeling in my stomach. Her breath smelt. Why? What causes that? I've noticed it a few times before but it's gone overboard now. It's happened too many times. Why can't it be fixed? I realise no girl will ever be flawless.'

He wrote about his girlfriend Annabel, her beauty and his fear that she would leave him. He was 'anxious' that others found her attractive and that she was aware of her allure. He had lost all confidence. His self-esteem was so low he now saw himself as a failure. His world had contracted into the small space in his head. He thought he was going mad.

'I don't know if anything is real. I'm unsure if what I think is good or what I'm told is good is really good. Maybe what is good is really bad and what is bad is really good.'

That would be the last sentence he would ever write, final thoughts—the thoughts we didn't hear.

From Christopher's diary: October 15th, 2001

Treat today as if you won't exist tomorrow.

OG MANDINO

chapter 9

There is a moment in everyone's life, a prophetic awakening when you instantly understand with the clarity of a sage what defines you, the reason for life itself. It's the fork in the road, the right or wrong path. It will change you, enlighten you, set you free or brand you forever. This was my moment as I stared down into Christopher's lidded eye sockets. I knew my life was over. I knew I couldn't live without my son.

It was Tuesday. Christopher had been dead for 110 hours. A shaft of lightning illuminated the divine figures huddled in prayer in the leadlight windows of the small suburban chapel. Thunder suspended the deathly silence and rattled the frames and the entry bars on the heavy, mahogany doors. In the distance a train arrived at the station then honked a slow departure.

We stood behind the closed doors—waiting.

I knew this would be the last time I would ever lay eyes on my son.

Two men in shiny black suits looked down respectfully as they signalled entry. Phil and I shuffled, hand in hand, down the short aisle, past empty pews and the sad floral arrangements from last Saturday's wedding. I looked up to the altar and stumbled as my legs locked. I couldn't walk, and Ben and Nic each took an arm and led me at a halting pace.

A photo of Jesus hung from the back wall, his gaze aimed at Christopher's lifeless body. We approached slowly then stared down at him with horror. His big, tanned hands, the only part of his body not gouged by the autopsy knife, were shrivelled and pasty. His large, muscly frame was brittle and had collapsed and shrunk like a two-day-old balloon.

The damage his brutal death caused had been masked with a white shroud, which I wasn't asked to choose. It concealed his twisted, broken leg and the livid bruises, stark upon his alabaster skin; the gaping wounds of the jagged rocks; his damaged organs, wrenched from their anchors, mingled in a thick, plastic bag in the vacuum of his eviscerated stomach. The hairline gash, sewn to conceal the gaping hole from which his brain had been cleaved from his spinal cord, was air-brushed with pasty makeup. It would never heal. His once-blond hair was dirty and limp and hung in dull strands over his sunken skull. That was not the way he wore it. His cheeks had collapsed under the weight of fractured bones and his full lips were now withered and thin. His sockets had shrunk to accommodate the prosthetic marbles, much smaller than the blue orbs I could stare into forever. He was the colour of concrete.

I bent down to kiss him—one last time. He was frigid and rigid and reeked of formaldehyde, not the familiar Giorgio Armani for Men Annabel had given to him for his sixteenth birthday. He wasn't there. He was a paper cut-out. He was someone else's son.

I collapsed, slithered to the floor like a deflating blow-up doll. Hands pulled at me, lifted me, dragged me away along the polished floorboards.

The doors closed behind our backs. The two black-suited men would take our son out of his coffin, put him back into his plastic womb and slide him into the steel morgue drawer. It would shut with a loud clank, rattling the corpses, the neighbours on either side. It would be cold and dark in there. He would be lonely. I wished I could be with him, lie with him, keep him warm. He didn't like to be cold; he hated to be alone and hated the dark.

I wished I had taken a lock of his hair.

We drove home in silence, Daisy at the wheel. Nic had an ear infection. I rang our doctor to order a prescription for antibiotics. Daisy pulled into the bottle shop in Avalon. Nic and I waited in the back seat. He pulled me to him and hugged me.

'You okay, Mum?'

I nodded then rested my head against the headrest.

'Don't worry. He's with God now.'

'I don't want him to be with God. I want him to be here with us.'

'You will be together again but you have to believe.'

'In what, Nic?'

'God. God says we are all reunited in death. Life isn't the end of the story. You have to find God, Mum, or we'll never be together again.'

I closed my eyes and sighed. How could I tell Nic I didn't want God, any god. I just wanted my son back. And how could I find God when I couldn't even find my feet?

chapter 10

The funeral: family and close friends gathered in the alcove of one of the many chapels at the Northern Suburbs Crematorium. I was sure it was the same one where we came to see my brother Jim before he was cremated. Christopher's coffin was by the altar, the gold crucifix ablaze in the early afternoon sunlight. I couldn't look at it and, yet, couldn't stop my mind picturing my son, hands clasped to chest in death's comedic pose in the dank carapace under the wooden lid. I had time. He was still whole. If I wanted to I could hold him, kiss him one more time. I could still get a lock of his hair.

Shore's reverend, Matthew Pickering, who would marry Ben and Sarah seven years later, stood at the lectern and cleared his throat. Christopher, he said, was a lovable, sensitive and vulnerable boy who often came to him for pastoral and spiritual guidance. When Christopher was in trouble, the reverend would try to find a way to help him. He told the congregation of the time Christopher came to school with dyed black hair and was thrown out of class by an exasperated maths teacher. Seeing him sitting outside the headmaster's office, Reverend Pickering rescued him and took him down the road to the barber for a short back and sides. I knew that Christopher idolised Reverend Pickering and there were many more rescues. But as Christopher started to drop out of life and eventually school, the contact became minimal.

I gripped my chair as a prayer was read. It was getting close to the end. I was frantic. How could I get someone to open the lid? I needed one more minute with him. I needed to hold him one more time. I needed to get his hair. I didn't have any scissors. Who would have scissors? My head was screaming. Time was running out ...

'When the boys were young,' Reverend Pickering continued, 'Jayne would kidnap them individually from their classrooms and take them to a fun place of their choice.'

He looked down over Christopher's coffin and then at me in the front-row pew and said: 'God has now kidnapped Christopher.'

I hated God then. How dare He presume?

We all stood to place white long-stemmed roses on top of the coffin then watched as it was wheeled to the automated furnace track. Someone in the back room pushed a button and the track clunked into gear. The coffin shuddered as it started the journey then suddenly stopped as though Christopher had changed his mind. I sucked in a mouthful of air and then, just as suddenly, it jerked forward towards the black velvet curtain. Then it disappeared. Gone. Over. Nothing. The space, the years, the love, the laughter had been replaced with an emptiness, as if his existence had been vacuumed into a dark vault where secret men did secret things which no one ever talked about. I wondered if they burned him straight away or waited till they finished their afternoon tea. As everyone slunk into waiting cars I stood and waited but could see no smoke from the chimney stack.

As we drove through the arched gates all I could think about was Christopher's cold flesh heating then melting, liquefying over his broken bones.

It would take ninety minutes at about 900 degrees centigrade. There would be nothing left but calcified bone fragments which would be pummelled by the machine equivalent of a mortar and pestle into something that resembled gritty ash. The final, traumatic assault. Dead end. One day he was here, the next evaporated as though he never existed at all. Photographs, trophies, Mother's Day cards and a bagful of ashes and bone particles—the only nebulous proof that I once had three sons.

I would take his ashes home because I wanted something tangible to touch, to look at. I put a teaspoon each in four little jewelled boxes so Phil, Ben and Nic could have something, too. We all keep them on our bedside tables.

The crematorium wanted me to put his ashes in a drawer, in a row, next to someone else's grandmother. I could visit whenever I wanted, a middle-aged woman with tight skin wearing a pink knitted twinset assured me.

I shook my head. I would be taking him home with me.

She gave me that look of pity and empowerment to which the non-grieving feel entitled. She pointed to a booklet of urn choices and, after I chose a simple black marble box, she asked what I wanted written on the plaque.

Christopher 'Cricket' Newling—22/10/1984 - 29/8/2002.

'Anything else?'

'That's all.'

I walked out among the manicured rows of the dead, the drawers, like spice compartments, layered and marked. Each drawer had its own little bud vase; most of them were empty, others receptacles for roses of every hue in various stages of decay. I was glad I wasn't leaving Christopher here among the neglected, perhaps long-forgotten dead.

I'd have to wait a week before his ashes were ready. Ben would collect the urn and bring it home for me, a duty I had performed for my parents when my brother smashed his motorbike into the back of a truck in 1984.

chapter 11

The memorial service: I opened my eyes as the sun shot a dagger through a gap in our bedroom curtains. Phil's side of the bed was empty; I could hear him talking to my friend Deby in the kitchen. The kettle whistled and I closed my eyes. If only I could have just lain here. If only I could have folded and melted into the sheets, evaporated like steam into the high corners of our lives. I didn't want to go to the service and have to face all those people. I didn't want everyone to acknowledge Christopher was really dead. Deby came in and sat on the bed, holding a steaming mug of tea.

'Drink!'

I closed my eyes and sighed.

'This is going to be a shit day,' she said. 'Somehow we're going to get through it. I'll be next to you all the way.'

'I just realised I don't have a dress. I have a plain white one and a blue one with flowers. I can't wear those. Shoes! Shit, I don't have any black shoes—except for my thongs and ugg boots. Why didn't I think of this? What am I going to do? There's not enough time. I can't do this, Deby.'

She told me to drink my tea and get dressed, she was taking me to Avalon and we would find something.

'We need a black dress,' Deby said to the shop assistant.

'Day or night wear?'

'Smart, not too fussy—and we don't have much time.'

The shop assistant sized me up, pulling three dresses from a rack.

'Special occasion?'

'No,' Deby spat. 'It's for a funeral.'

'This will do,' I said, throwing the unwanted two over the back of a chair.

'Don't you want to try it on?'

'It will fit.'

'She hates shopping,' Deby grimaced. 'She never tries anything on.'

There were four pairs of black sandals in the shoe shop window.

'Which one?' I asked.

Deby pointed to a pair. We ran in and bought my size without trying them on either.

At home Deby, a hairdresser, helped me with my lank hair. I tried to dress myself but my hands were sweaty and shaking. She lifted me from the bed and hugged my shuddering body. She took off my tracksuit then slowly pulled the dress over my head, clipped my stockings and shod my feet. It was time to go.

There were cards and large bouquets attached to the school's front gates. Crowds milled at the edges of the long driveway. Hundreds of chairs, like the tombstones of unknown soldiers, dotted the lawn. A sound system had been erected for the benefit of those who could not squeeze into the large chapel. Fifteen hundred people came to say goodbye to Cricket. Our family was the last to be led down the aisle. A floral arrangement in the shape of a nine, Christopher's rugby number, was propped against the lectern. That was Murgy's mum Trish's gift to me. Phil gripped me fiercely to steady my shaking legs.

We sat near the front. I stared down at my stupid black sandals with their sensible heel and counted to ten, then backwards, then to twenty and backwards, until I got to a hundred; then I started all over again.

A prayer was read, a psalm was sung. And then his name was mentioned. *Cricket.* I clenched my fists and willed myself to stay strong.

Headmaster Grant delivered the main eulogy, followed by Phil's father Graham who bravely read on our behalf.

Then it was Ben's turn. My heart broke as he resolutely strode to the altar. I was amazed by his courage to get up before so many people and talk about his brother in such a raw and honest way. He spoke with a trembling despair about his pride for his brother but also the regret that, while they were so close growing up, they weren't at the end of Christopher's life because they battled over responsibilities.

'Cricket was at times a troubled kid who was always searching for his place in the world,' Ben said. 'He found solace through his friends and rugby. We had our problems during our teenage years but I always loved him. I only hope he knew that. I had looked forward to the time when we would both be adults and our relationship would improve through our maturity. I only wish I still had that chance.'

I couldn't look at him as he took his seat. My brave, responsible, sensitive, loving, devastated son.

At the last minute, Nic couldn't read his eulogy but stood close to Reverend Pickering as he took over.

'When I was lonely, Criddy let me hang out with him and his buddies. When I was bullied, he protected me along with eighty-five of his mates. He always looked out for his little brother and I wouldn't give him the satisfaction of admitting it but I really did look up to him. I admired him. I wanted to be him.'

Nic asked everyone not to mourn his brother but to 'pick up the same Bible which Criddy did—read Mark—learn God's word. Then one day we will all be together again with Criddy.'

I lowered my head as another prayer was read. This was savage, so silent and surreal. We should be screaming, punching walls, throwing angry fists at the face of God, smiling down on us in glorious, leadlight colours. Our deeds should match the anger surging and blistering a pathway through our veins.

Then suddenly it was over. Silence. Still as fear. Faces blurred, voices muffled and fell to the floor. Everyone stood with bowed heads as we made our way outside. Christopher's rugby team formed a guard of honour. I wanted to go to them, to thank them on Christopher's behalf for being such great friends, but we couldn't move from the doorway. For more than an hour, we stood in the cold, hugging each person as they came out of the chapel. No one seemed to want to leave.

The sun was just beginning to set behind North Sydney's skyscrapers, enveloping the chapel with a rose-tinged aura. Phil put his arm around me and I smiled with exhaustion. Antony Weiss hugged me, as did Reverend Pickering, Bob Grant and Graham Robertson, and on behalf of the entire school, these four men, who had tried so hard to save our son, presented us with the school flag.

That night I threw the dress and shoes into the garbage bin.

chapter 12

~~~

Silence enveloped us in the days and weeks after the funeral. It wasn't just a blanket of grief but the white shock of disbelief. Glazed and disorientated we floated in and out of every minute like zombies. Silence was hushed except in my mind. While nothing was said, a look that lingered a second more than was comfortable, or a hug which shackled me to an acquaintance, made my mind explode. The throbbing rhythms of pain and pity played on and on and on. People drifted in and out, leaving food, clawing at a memory or taking something of Christopher's to 'remember him by'—a photograph, a T-shirt, a book or his ring.

And as they left they'd drop a seed of wisdom into the potted fig by the front door, wishing it would take root overnight to give us hope and to straighten our backs.

'It's not your fault.'

'I know it was an accident—I'm sure Cricket wouldn't take his own life.'

'If he did, you have to believe it was his choice.'

Guilt likes to write all over you, press you flat then encase you in an envelope with a lavish lick. And when you've been tossed and slotted and forgotten, it is guilt which will throw a return party in your honour. Guilt can kill you. It will chortle and rebuke you for not being able to save your son.

That was when the hate began—self-hate. I felt isolated, even from Phil, Ben and Nic, and I watched and waited for others to hate me, too. I couldn't save their brother, their friend, their boyfriend, Phil's son. Christopher's death cut me in half and I knew my life was over.

I pushed everyone away so I wouldn't see the disappointment mirrored in their eyes. If I couldn't stop Christopher, how would I stop Nic?

A few weeks after Christopher died I sent Phil, Ben and Nic to grief counsellors. It was the only practical thing I could think of to help them. I couldn't be a mother and take care of Nic physically and emotionally and I was scared I'd make him want to die, too. And I couldn't be a wife. I didn't want to be touched, soothed, fondled. I didn't want to sleep in the same bed with Phil and I didn't want to make love—ever again.

If I gave in to my grief I knew I'd be letting go of Christopher, bit by bit; the sound of his voice, the taste of sea salt on his neck, the smell of his Giorgio Armani. If the death of a child is the stab wound, grief is the first suture; acceptance, the salve. I wanted none of it. I wanted to keep him alive. Grief was his death certificate which I shoved at the back of my drawer with the paperclips and rubber bands.

Christopher was in every room; on the blue vinyl couch where he languished one night too drunk to trek up the stairs, in the sunroom where he asked me to wax his legs so he could run faster, on my bedroom wall where, on the night after he died, a cricket chirped and chirped until I fell asleep and it expired. In the morning, and hoping I hadn't noticed, Phil scooped it up and buried it in the garden.

For what is it to die but to stand naked in the wind
and melt into the sun?
And what is it to cease breathing, but to free the breath
from its restless tides, that it may rise and expand and
seek God unencumbered?
Only when you drink from the river of silence shall you indeed sing.
And when you have reached the mountain top, then
You shall begin to climb
And when the earth shall claim your limbs, then you
Shall truly dance

KAHLIL GIBRAN, FROM 'ON DEATH'

chapter 13

~

Most suicidal people are undecided about whether they really want to live or die. Sometimes when they attempt suicide they are gambling with death, and leave it to others to save them.

FROM THE *THE CRUELEST DEATH: THE ENIGMA OF ADOLESCENT SUICIDE*
BY DAVID LESTER PHD, A LEADING AUTHORITY ON SUICIDE

By the time you finish reading this chapter, someone in the world will have overdosed on heroin, jumped off a cliff, drowned in the ocean, thrown themselves in front of a train, asphyxiated under a plastic bag, shoved a gun into their mouth, cut their wrists, thrown a hairdryer in a bathtub or hanged themselves. Nearly one million people suicide every year and that's only the documented, known cases. That is more than those murdered, killed in war or on the roads. In Australia, more than two thousand people take their own lives and even that number is probably conservative as many suicides go unreported—like Christopher's.

His cause of death: massive head injury. The coroner could not ascertain whether he jumped or fell and because he left no suicide note he is not, like many others, a suicide statistic.

When a parent loses a child through an illness, accident or even murder, the grief lasts a lifetime. Their only comfort perhaps is that their child wanted to live. For Phil and me and thousands of other parents of children who suicide, not only do we have to grieve their death and deal with the sudden vacuum it has left in our lives, but there's the guilt and shame that they wanted to die. Parents want and need to protect their children.

When you fail, you lose everything—your self-esteem, confidence, the ability to love and to care, and the will to live and to fight for life. The signs of wanting to die are often there but, in many cases, only after your child has killed himself. It's an insidious secret. They're not going to tell anyone and even if asked, it will almost always be denied. If a parent knew the intention, the suicide may be prevented.

Any sudden death is shocking. It's the randomness of it—a heart attack or being hit by a car. But suicide is inexplicable and more horrifying in that a choice is made, a decision which in an instant could be reversed.

No one wants to talk about suicide. It always has been, and still is to some extent, a family's dirty secret. In the Middle Ages not only was a person who died by his own hand not allowed a proper burial, his body was disgraced. It would be dragged through the streets, his head placed on a pole outside the city gates as a warning to others.

Suicide became a topic of social interest between the seventeenth and eighteenth centuries. This was reflected most palpably by Shakespeare's works, where a host of his characters including Romeo and Juliet, Othello and Brutus died at their own hands. Famous people, such as Vincent Van Gogh, Mark Antony, Cleopatra, Virginia Woolf, Kurt Cobain, all committed suicide. There have been suggestions that Marilyn Monroe and Elvis Presley committed suicide but no one will ever know for certain. Many Jews imprisoned at Treblinka, one of the most notorious World War 2 Nazi concentration camps, chose to suicide as an affirmation of the freedom to control their own destiny.

In 1897, French sociologist Emile Durkheim published the first scientific study of suicide—*Le Suicide*—in which he argued that suicide was not just an individual choice. He suggested society as a contributing factor.

Then Sigmund Freud introduced the world to the concept of psychosis and suggested mental disorders were medical conditions. This helped pave the way for changes in civil, criminal and religious laws concerning suicide. Most European countries formally decriminalised suicide in the eighteenth and nineteenth centuries, although it remained a crime in England and Wales until 1961 and in Ireland until 1993. It was only in 1983 that the Roman Catholic Church reversed the canon law that prohibited funeral rites and burial in church cemeteries for those who had suicided.

~~

Who knew Christopher was suicidal? I should have known. He was my son. Inside my head questions zoom in circles, round and round again. I can hear them. What if I loved him harder? What if I talked to him more? What if I had him committed to a mental institution? It never stops and probably never will. It stops when I close my eyes at night but sometimes, in my dreams, the questions return, only posed by a visual horror.

I'm on one side of a thick floor-to-ceiling glass panel in one recurring nightmare. It separates my bedroom from the hallway and beyond. Christopher is a toddler and is banging his fists repeatedly on the glass wall. Something or someone is trying to get to him, to kill him. I can't see what it is but I know I don't have much time. I jump out of bed and try to break the glass. I hit the wall with my fists, I bash it with the rocking chair, drawers from my bedside table. The glass is impenetrable and the more I throw at it, the more distressed Christopher becomes. He's screaming at me to help him, to save him. I watch helplessly as he is dragged away. I always wake up screaming.

It took two weeks to receive Christopher's death certificate and a further five months for his autopsy report. I hoped there would be something to give me doubt it was a suicide.

Phil didn't want to know any details. It was as if he had shut down. He didn't want to question the friends who were with Christopher that night, or give a statement to police. He didn't ask about the coroner's findings and has never asked to see the autopsy report. For him, he had lost his son and nothing would change that. That is a common reaction for many parents, but for others, like me, every detail had to be combed through, every question asked and answered. Maybe I had hoped I'd find a reason. Maybe he was drunk and he slipped or the paramedics didn't do their job.

When the autopsy report was finally delivered, I locked myself into my bedroom and slowly read through the thirteen pages. Unable to understand most of it, I made an appointment with Dr Eccles, who gently explained all the medical jargon.

This is what I understood. His body was cold to touch and rigor mortis was present and lividity (the black and blue of congealed blood) had developed on his back. After death, when the circulation stops, blood pools, discolouring the skin. He had blood in his ears, nose and mouth and his body was covered in bruises. His brain weighed 1420 grams and due to the extensive head injury, his brain was placed in formalin for further investigation.

I didn't know when I saw him at the funeral home that his head was empty.

His lungs were filled with blood. He had paracetamol, codeine and venlafaxine, an antidepressant, in his blood. He had a bandaid on his fourth and fifth fingers on his left hand and his right leg was broken. His brain had been torn away from his spinal cord. He had no chance.

There is no grief like the grief that does not speak.

HENRY WADSWORTH LONGFELLOW

chapter 14

As I sit down to write about the death of my son, the first claws of autumn rip the air 1000 metres above sea level. It is March, 2013. In five months Christopher will have been dead for eleven years. Outside my study window in Sydney's Blue Mountains, the mist has rolled in, blanketing the tall rhododendron and magnolia trees. The king parrots and rosellas are dining out on the last of the crab apple pods and the black cockatoos, having annihilated the pine cones, screech high overhead searching for a winter hideaway.

It is cold enough to light a fire in the hundred-year-old hearth and as it warms my back I feel the first tentacles of despair, the wretchedness which rubs up against me like an unwanted dog, its faecal residue lingering long after I finish for the day. I rub the back of my neck, let my fingers undulate in an upward motion between the vertebrae and stop at the spot where I think the brain attaches to the spinal cord. I strike it with the side of my hand like an axe. My head jars and my brain jangles, sending spikes of ice needles to my eyeballs. My brain resettles and I open my eyes. It takes three seconds to see clearly again. It takes the same amount of time to fall 10 metres off a cliff and a fraction of that for 'injuries sustained to be incompatible with life'.

At the end of writing this chapter today I'll have a headache, diarrhoea and a heart which feels lined with viscous tar. It is a purge with no clear benefits.

I look down the long, dark tunnel of grief and wonder why it still sits on me, heavy like a dead animal. Haven't I done my time? Can I not be given back my wings and like the dragonfly, the devil's darning needle, knit myself back into this world as it was before Christopher changed our happy lives?

This is the first time I've said that, the first time I've thrown blame at his feet. I want to take it back, rewrite it, but just for today, that's how I feel. Grief has gouged much deeper lines than age would normally allow between Phil's eyes, those soft and moist brown orbs which have lost the gleam of a life well-lived and the sparkle of an anticipatory future. And me? My skin hangs in disappointed folds and I cannot hear the music because I no longer care to dance. Ben can't talk about Christopher, not even to Sarah, who is now his wife. He is safe behind his milky veneer but I know his heart lies in a tenuous, vaulted chamber which an ache would open and streak him with another jagged scar.

And Nic? After all the drugs and perhaps because of the ECT, much of his mid-term memory is fractured. It upsets him that he can't remember Christopher as clearly as he would like. He has begged me for years to write about him, a gift, he says, which would 'give me back the memory of Criddy'. For him, his brother is ghost-like, a caricatured jigsaw of images and memories.

Last weekend I gave him the first two chapters to read and left him slouched in a cane chair on the front balcony. My heart broke as I watched him from my study window, struggling with the words. And then, when I saw his tears bulge and swell like an engorged balloon then drop onto page one, chapter one, a loud sob shook me, the sudden pain as quick and shocking as a wasp bite. He stroked away the tears with a single swipe as I sat down beside him, waiting for him to finish.

'It's good, Mum. Please keep writing.'

I held him and cried into his mane of blond, greasy hair. I felt a mixture of pride and guilt as I made him a promise to finish what I'd started.

Unlike Ben, Nic often talks about Christopher but it's from a feeling, a distant notion of the aura surrounding the brother who captivated him, the brother he can hardly remember.

Many of Christopher's friends still protect Nic, mostly because they loved their mate and perhaps, like us, feel a shame they didn't have the chance to save him. They tell Nic stories, naughty tales of Christopher's mischievousness. They remind him of how he could always 'pull a chick' or light up a room. If Christopher wore a particular T-shirt, that was the new fashion. Everyone surfed with the same board and chose to curl the sides of their caps like Christopher did with his. Many of these friends support Nic, donating money to the Black Dog Institute's annual fundraiser. Every year, Nic and a group, usually associated with mental health, trek some part of the world to raise awareness and funds for Black Dog. Nic has trekked the Great Wall Of China, Machu Picchu in Peru and the mountaintops in the kingdom of Bhutan. He has worked for Black Dog for four years, setting up and managing BITE BACK, a positive psychology website to help teenagers build resilience. He continues his enthusiasm for speaking to teenagers at various Sydney high schools, openly discussing his mental illness, the devastating effect of his brother's suicide and his fight for recovery. It is his life's passion—suicide awareness and prevention.

This is the positive side to our family's trauma but it is only one square in the quilt of our grief; those tiny, perfect sections of different fabrics sewn together in a mishmash of prints and hues. It is a well-loved heirloom when seen all at once but an eyesore when you try to make some sense of the patchwork landscape. If I hold it to me it feels warm but then it prickles against my naked heat and I have to lay it down for more practical uses.

If I named each square with an encapsulating epithet, it would read like an angry lament which no one would care to decipher. It would feel like ice over the helpless mound of the homeless man slumped in the doorway of God's cathedral.

Every day, I hug it and tuck it and fold it away. The senselessness of it all—the damage—the unending angst three seconds can cause. It lurks on every surface, behind every closed door and around each corner. It's there like a muse atop my shoulder and in my outdoor shadow it frolics along to a melodic four-four beat. And just when I think I've leashed it and tied it to the dungeon door, I will see Nic cry or Ben battle against a memory. I will see Phil redden, close his eyes and choke on a ball of grief too large to swallow. Even now, after more than a decade of trying to live with this pall of misery, I realise the surface is merely sprinkled with a fine sheath of dust penetrable by the sun, the moon or a thunderstorm. Just the whisper of his name will make my heart contract.

The long, sad journey of the years has wearied us all, made us watchful, vigilant, fearful of what could happen next. Can lightning strike twice? Is it discriminate? Do I fear for my sons? Yes, every day. Will Nic have a car crash, will Ben hit his head on his skiff's boom, become unconscious and drown? Will Phil have a heart attack?

And does Ben look at his one-year-old son, Zach, and give thanks that he is healthy and happy, or is he frightened he may lose him one day, like Phil and I did, like my mother and father did?

This is the journey of grief. And even after eleven years it still can incapacitate you, eviscerate you, suck you dry then spit you out like an unwanted wad of glutinous meat. It can send you mad. It feels like an illness, a prolonged cancer, for which there is no cure.

There is a pill to deaden it or a bottle of wine to quieten it for a little while, but it's always there in the morning.

Still, now, grief is the dread which wakens me. Christopher's face is my day's first image and his death, the horribleness of it, the slow-motion intricacies of his final breath, is what wakes me in the middle of the night, shuddering, frightened. Still. Now.

Grief is an enemy. It assails you, hits you, batters you blue. It's a torturer, slow and cruel. The last thing you think about when your child is born is that he may die before you. And when he does, the shock of it fries you. It marks the moments of each day like a thorn on a rose bush just around the corner, and when you are least prepared, it stabs. Reminders of his favourite things, the taste of a strawberry guava, Eminem, a rugby match or a smile from one of his friends. Or it can be a photograph of him, in a room I hadn't entered in a while. I study his seventeen-year-old smiling face and wonder what he would look like now. Had the seeds of depression and anxiety already altered him, damaged him, made up his mind for him?

Still, now, I wonder what I could have done. I still crave to go back in time, pull him to me and bash out the illness that made him want to die more than to live and fight. This insidious, secretive, destructive illness so severe that life was too painful for him to endure. And while he may have teetered for a time between the alternatives, at exactly 11:30 on the night of August 29th, 2002, it was an exhausted, frightened, desperate teenager who tossed the coin in the air but didn't wait for it to land.

Watching your son die, alone, cold and unable to hear any comforting words, would send any parent mad. There were times, in the early years, when my body fell to the floor and no one could pick me up. I wanted to melt into the cold tiles, evaporate into nothingness. I wanted to be with Christopher, wherever that was, for who can say for sure where the dead live?

I would have gladly forsaken everything, my husband, my sons, to be numb, to be dead. I would stand on the same precipice and, in the glow of the floodlight erected by council to prevent other suicides, tempt myself with the ignoble glory of oblivion. I could throw myself over it or force my feet into a backward shuffle to thwart the throbbing impulse. Forward, back, forward, back.

A week after Christopher's death I stood there, watching the moon scribble on the ocean's tides. I was frozen, my senses alive and alert. I could smell the seaweed, hear the flap of the wings of some nocturnal bird and taste the salt in the frigid air. A new floodlight blazed the rock face and the ocean pool below. On the fence railing just behind me, his friends had painted: RIP Cricket—forever loved by all who knew you. 22/10/1984 – 29/8/2002. Every day I would go to that fence and run my hands along the rough letters. Being there made me feel closer to him, in some esoteric way; but then several weeks later, the council painted over it and it felt like another death.

I stared down at the spot where Christopher's body landed and wondered if I manoeuvred my body, whether I'd be able to hit the same spot.

Then I suddenly understood everything. At this very instant, when life meant nothing, when pain had cauterised every nerve ending, I knew how easy it would be to let go. It would only take a second. I knew then my son's last thought and I understood that with the snap of fingers it was over, but for us, for everyone who loved him, we are sentenced to a lifetime to consider the consequences.

Still I stood there, teetering. Forward, back, forward, back.

Then everything went black and the shock of it took my breath away. I looked up to the floodlight and watched as it sucked in the last of its glow like the fade-out on a movie screen. I jumped back over the railing and shuffled down the hill to make my way home, wondering why the floodlight went out just before midnight.

~

A flash of memory. Christopher laughing, a steaming baked chicken, a surfboard and runny spaghetti. He was fifteen. Spaghetti was his favourite, especially the way Anne, Matt Holmes's mum, made it.

'Yours has lumps in it,' he said to me as he loomed over the pot with a wooden spoon. 'Mrs Holmes's spaghetti is smooth and runny but thick. How does she do that?'

'I don't know,' I answered with mock irritation. 'Why don't you ask her?'

He smiled then hugged me tight as he always did when he wanted to smooth my annoyance. He patted me on the back playfully then returned to the dining room where three of his mates were grabbing at a slab of garlic bread. I put the meat sauce into the blender and whirled and pulsed it until there were no more lumps. I poured it over the pasta, sprinkled a handful of parmesan cheese on top and set it in the middle of the table with a triumphant 'tah-dah'. They looked at each other then burst into laughter as the liquefied sauce leaked over the plate's lip and into the extender crack of my mother-in-law's Jacobean dining table, onto the newly laid cream carpet. Murgy gave me a hug saying how delicious it looked. The others were giggling like little girls and I told them so. I never made spaghetti again.

These memories, the good and bad, crush me, the weight of them. Too heavy, oppressive like a crowded lift. It takes a long time to get to know grief, to understand it. It is like a lonely, unwanted friend who brings cupcakes and settles herself beside your fire, sipping tea with empathy. You want to strangle it, beat it, toss it on the funeral pyre. But you can never grab hold of it; it's always just past your reach.

~

Grief is a pain, a stab wound which reopens with each day's awakening. Without you realising, it defines you. Everything you were before is gone. The happy you, loving you, funny you, interesting you.

For a long time I felt like a morose, bitter and dried wastrel going about banal duties I resented, the weight of it electrocuting my nerves. I still had two children, everyone was anxious to remind me, but my arms felt empty. There was no going back. I couldn't say I'm sorry, I've made a mistake, I'll do it right this time. Robbed of that, life felt like a prison sentence. Grief was the enemy within my soul. It assailed me, hit me, battered me and it always wore a smile. My heart was broken and for many years I felt I couldn't live without Christopher. I couldn't bear the thought of never seeing him again. I couldn't look at the photos Phil wanted to keep in every room. I didn't want to open my eyes in the morning and I couldn't wait to close them at night. I felt resentment that with each dawn the sun insisted on rising. It should have rained, thundered, hailed. I naively thought that after the viewing, the cremation, the memorial service and after my house had emptied and I could be alone again, this thing called grief, the razor edge of this deep pain, would soften and, given enough time, lie just behind memory in a milky bubble. I didn't know then that I'd be in shock for years and that by avoiding grief, it would send me mad.

I would look at Ben and Nic and my guilt and shame would crush me. I felt numb and a stranger in their hearts. They still hugged me—all the time—just in case. They held me because they didn't want to let me go. They would tell me they loved me to cement me to this life. Phil's grief was palpable but he was better than me at getting through a day. He could touch hope, strive for his survival. Life still had meaning for him. He broke down many times but then he'd suddenly smile at a memory—'beautiful memories', he'd tell me.

'Remember the time when Christopher...'

I couldn't and I didn't want to then. I was angry. Angry at the buzz saw destroying my solitude, angry when the phone rang, angry when I dropped a lettuce leaf on the floor and would have to decide whether to wash it or throw it in the compost bin. I was angry when a queue of ants wound their way around the curved back of the Buddha in Christopher's memorial garden.

I was pinned between misery and responsibility and the inanity of constant advice. I knew I had two other sons but that didn't fuse the fissure in my heart. It was just another avenue of guilt.

I would be fine if everyone had left me alone. I would be okay because I had two other sons and a husband who would probably end up hating me. I'd be fine as long as I could be alone and for as long as I could pretend that I wasn't insane. I would be fine if the phone would stop ringing and I sprayed the ants; fine, if I could hold on to a lettuce leaf.

But now I know grief. Time has, in some ways, eased the torment, but the melancholia of loss never leaves you. It bubbles deep down within but is flat and inert just under the first layer of skin. No one can live with that early, shocking grief. To survive you have to find a way to live with it, allow it in and then close the door behind it—just long enough to breathe.

As I made my way home from the headland a week after Christopher's death, grief was just a word.

I closed the front door behind me, quickly undressed and slipped into bed quietly. Phil was sleeping peacefully on his back. I searched for his hand in the dark and knitted my fingers through his. He squeezed my hand tightly. I felt so sorry for him, this wonderful, gentle, loving, kind father. I knew he would never recover from this. I knew our marriage would probably not survive. I knew I could never love him or anyone else again. Anger and bitterness would consume us and we would end up battling our demons on our own.

chapter 15

We were married on July 3rd, 1981, in an historic church on Phillip Street in the heart of Sydney. I was twenty-three and Phil was a year older. We met at high school when I was just fifteen and despite a couple of dramatic, angst-filled teenage splits, we always knew that we'd get married and have children. I was attracted to his gentleness, morality and sense of humour and although he was an inch shorter than me, I perfected the art of bending my knees just a little to give the appearance we were of complementary height. He was a gentleman who always opened my car door, and still does. He was smart and loving and protective. When another man looked at me, he'd eyeball them then wrap a possessive arm around my shoulder. I'd never been loved in this way. When I asked him recently what attracted him to me, he said my thighs.

'Be serious,' I said mock-punching him on the arm.

'I am.'

I did have big thighs. I was a sprinter and played hockey. The school's rugby players would tease me that they were jealous of my masculine bulging muscles. Phil played rugby. We cemented our romance on an interschool sporting exchange with a Canberra school. He'd watch me play hockey and I'd watch his rugby matches. We'd sneak out each night from our billeted families and meet by Canberra's War Memorial. He'd walk me back and kiss me one more time as I snuck through an open window.

'Was there anything else you liked about me?' I prodded again.

'Nuh.'

'Really?'

'No, nothing.'

As I write this chapter an email notification from Phil lights up my screen—the subject: What attracted me to you.

'Besides your athletic legs, it was your blond hair that flew on the slightest breeze and your big blue eyes ... like a doll. I never had the guts to talk to you but that's how I saw you before we met.'

He wrote that after we met: 'It was your quietness, almost aloofness that intrigued me. I found out that those character traits didn't come from arrogance or confidence but a lack of those qualities. You had a great sense of humour but because of your lack of confidence it was kept under wraps. As we got to know each other, it came out more. I'd never met a girl who liked poetry. You read it and wrote it—usually dark. You introduced me to Kahlil Gibran. You had a great capacity to love and when it came my way, it was powerful and deep. I had not felt such love before. It distracted me from most things around me and that's when I fell in love with you.'

'Good enough,' I replied by email.

It was during one of our break-ups when he called to ask me out for dinner. I was living with a girlfriend in a two-bedroom flat in Kirribilli. I had just arrived home from an arduous hockey game with older girls from North Sydney. I was covered in mud and bruises. I said yes and threw myself under the shower.

He turned up at seven and we walked to a romantic French restaurant around the corner. Several years later it was renamed and rejigged into a girlie, lap-sitting, burlesque eatery of questionable distinction.

That night, during dessert, he said he never wanted to be separated from me again and asked me to marry him.

The following year, wearing the ivory satin and lace dress my grandmother had made for my mother's wedding, I made Phil a promise to love him until the day I die.

Eighteen months into our marriage Ben was born, followed by Christopher twenty-one months later, then Nic another twenty-one months after that. Three boys under four. Immediately after delivering Nic, I tried to get off the high delivery bed but a severe leg cramp forced me to lie back down. While I grimaced in agony, Phil was smiling, humming to the tune of *My Three Sons*.

It was a hectic time, raising three boys mostly on my own and trying to hold on to my freelance career. I was generally exhausted, especially during the numerous bouts of teething, colds and flu and ear infections. But my love for them was so powerful it hurt. When Ben was a baby I couldn't imagine being able to love another child as much as him.

When Jim died, Ben didn't understand why I cried at night. I cried deep and hard for my baby brother. My parents received the same advice as I would eighteen years later—'At least you have other children.' His death made me fear losing my only son. Phil and I agreed to have another child. I went off the contraceptive pill, thinking it might take six months to fall pregnant, but Christopher was conceived straight away, as if he couldn't wait or feared we may change our minds. Ten days late and weighing a little over four kilos, he was forced into this world through induction and forceps.

Twelve months later I fell pregnant with Nic unexpectedly. Although the thought crossed our minds at the time that we were both tired and feared we couldn't afford a third child, Phil and I both cried and hugged each other when it was decided we would definitely keep our baby. I had visions of Ben and Christopher sitting under the Christmas tree with a vacant space between them, like someone no longer in favour being cut from a photograph. Nic arrived in a hurry, weighing over four and a half kilos. From the beginning he was anxious to get into life.

Although they all had similar features they had very different personalities, but they were all kind and loving and polite. On one of our home videos Christopher demanded more soap.

'Cricket, you should say, may I have more soap, please,' Ben chastised.

'May I have some more soap, please, Mama,' Christopher duly obeyed.

Ben was soft and patient with his two baby brothers. He would unbutton Christopher's shirts before he was able to do it himself and always undressed Nic for the nightly bath. One video captured Ben and Christopher practising tackles in our small lounge room and then Nic, at one, and unaware he was being watched, climbing up onto the kitchen bench trying to work out how voices came out of the radio. Pan back to the lounge room and Christopher had just performed a drop-knee tackle on Ben. Ben rolled away in agony; Christopher hugged him and apologised.

During that same period when Christopher was four, he was at Little Nippers on a Sunday morning with his best friend Laurie who was trying to puncture a bluebottle which had washed up on the shore. Christopher was yelling at him not to kill it.

'Don't pop it, don't pop it,' he screamed at Laurie.

When Laurie continued, Christopher pushed him hard enough for him to fall into the surf.

'Don't do it! Never,' Christopher said with tears in his eyes. 'Never, never.'

We have many happy videos of our young sons but up until recently, I haven't been able to watch them. I was locked into the bad times, the sad memories. I was frightened that if I saw Christopher alive, I'd lose my mind. Phil had encouraged me for years to watch them and when I finally did, he sat with me and held my hand as I laughed at their antics and marvelled at their beauty and innocence. He held me tight as I wept while watching Christopher hug me and whisper something in my ear.

This was our happy, hectic, funny, adventurous, beautiful family. I read them books, I taught them songs, colours and the alphabet. Phil taught them honesty and decency and how to tackle around the knees. We loved them with physical and emotional abandon. Ben loved to wrap his arms around my neck and kiss me hard on the cheek, Nic liked to rub noses, and Christopher would grab my cheeks and rub his lips over mine and say 'moochie, moochie'. Nic loved Superman, Cricket loved Batman and Ben loved Robin.

Of course they grew into robust teenagers but their intrinsic, sweet, kind and caring natures stayed with them. That was until Ben at sixteen got depression, followed closely by Christopher and Nic. That's when my happy, hectic, funny, adventurous, beautiful family fell apart.

From Christopher's diary: November 22nd, 2001

Half-way up the hill I see the Past
Lying beneath me with its sounds and sights,
A city in the twilight dim and vast,
With smoking roofs, soft bells, and gleaming lights,
And hear above me on the autumnal blast
The cataract of Death far thundering from the heights.

HENRY WADSWORTH LONGFELLOW

chapter 16

~

In the weeks following the funeral, I went back to the headland every day looking for answers. To even begin to understand why Christopher died I had to find out what happened that night. It would take me months to piece most of it together.

Ray, a gentle, robust policeman with a brief smile and eyes which had seen too much, was willing to help me. He was the officer in charge and had been there on August 29th.

It was a warm, September day—lunchtime. Ray drove me to Avalon Beach, parked his police car by the surf club and helped me across the sand. Mothers and their toddlers sat on beach towels eating fish and chips, young women oiled flawless skin and suntanned surfers with waxed boards waited at the water's edge for the tide to turn.

We were a spectacle, Ray in his uniform, I in jeans, as their gazes followed us to the ocean pool. We walked around the safety fence and Ray knelt, inviting me to join him. I stared at the hard rock surface looking for any traces of blood but there was nothing; it was just a rock which had been moulded over the centuries by an often tempestuous sea. Little black crabs darted out of the chiselled holes and, spying unwanted guests, scurried back to safety. I looked up at the sheer cliff face, the jagged ledges carpeted with tussocks of brown grass. Clumps of asparagus fern and seaside daisies sprouted indiscriminately through the cracks in the rock and at the very top, a lone gum tree struggled on a thin and shaky trunk battling against the raging coastal elements.

'Has that floodlight always been there?' I asked Ray.

He shook his head and hesitated.

'No. The council erected it after ...' He paused then sighed. 'A few weeks ago.'

'Because of Christopher?'

He nodded. 'Hopefully it will save others,' he whispered.

He gazed at me deeply as he gently shook his head from side to side.

'I'm sorry,' he said, wrapping his big, blue policeman's arm around my shoulders. And then I cried and he pulled me to him, holding me tightly until my body stilled.

'Where did it happen? Exactly.'

Ray pointed to a ledge 10 metres above our heads then down to the rock where we were standing. I sat down. Ray hovered over me, his body bent, his arms like wings encircling a newly hatched fledgling. We stayed there for a while, frozen statues lost in thought.

Then he lifted me and guided me back along the beach to the car park, to the spot where the ambulance had been parked. I looked out to the ocean where Christopher used to surf. The board riders had paddled out behind a set of bulging waves and at the water's edge, two small children squealed as pools of foam broke over their toes. They ran back to their sand holes and threw themselves in, scattering sand in every direction. Their mother smiled as she tried to slap their squirming bodies with sunscreen. My skin bristled with envy. How I wished I was her. At the end of this day, she'd pack up her picnic, towels, buckets and spades and her children. She'd bathe them then make tacos. All warm and soft and smelling of lavender, she'd read them a story, maybe even 'Elfie', then kiss and cuddle them while she wrapped them into bed for the night. Tomorrow would be another day. She'd wake, like I used to, full of hope and fun and plans. Every day would be just like this one, every year marked off with a new achievement, another birthday, the Easter bunny and Santa. Their heights would be measured with a pencil line behind the kitchen door, their weight by the number of piggyback rides she could endure.

That's how it was meant to be. That's how it was for Phil and me. Every morning and one by one, wearing their favourite 'jammies', their little chubby bodies would shuffle down the hall. With matted hair and rubbing sleep from their eyes, they'd dive onto the couch for a quick cuddle before breakfast. Ben and Christopher would wrestle while Nic 'helped' in the kitchen. I couldn't have known then that this perfect life would fall apart, that mental illness would all but destroy my family. We had three beautiful, healthy, happy, intelligent boys who would grow up to be beautiful, happy, healthy, successful adults. Ben wanted to be a fireman; Christopher, a famous rugby player; Nic, an 'animal fixer' (veterinarian).

How I wish I could go back twelve years, stare madness in the face and banish it from our home. Perhaps I should have asked its name, befriended it, calmed and cajoled it, invited it in for dinner. Maybe that's why madness didn't care. I left it out in the dark, hungry, lonely and cold.

chapter 17

Time is free, but it's priceless. You can't own it, but you can use it. You can't keep it but you can spend it. Once you've lost it, you can never get it back.

HARVEY MACKAY, AUTHOR AND BUSINESS LEADER

One hour. One long hour to save Christopher's life. But we weren't given the chance. At the end of that hour, it would be too late.

In her statement to the police, Ally said: 'Chris stayed with me on most occasions since January [2002]. He told me he suffered depression and anxiety. He took tablets every day to ease his anxiety. In the last two weeks, Chris stayed at my place every night. In March, a friend of his committed suicide and Chris found this very difficult to deal with. He spoke about suicide. Sometimes he was opposed to it and then he would change his mind. On August 29th, we spent the day together. We watched a video but he got upset because he was alone for a short time. He hated being alone. Chris was writing a letter. I thought it was for me but he told me it was for his psychologist who told him to write his feelings down. I don't know where this letter went.'

~~

I don't know what else Christopher did on the day of his death. I know that after he was with Ally he was alone until he went to rugby training with Jack. They were late and were berated by the coach who ordered extra sprints after training. That night, while we were at Nic's school play, Christopher came home and changed then drove to Jack's house for a barbecue. I know he ate a steak and sausage and the autopsy report showed that he drank enough to give him a mid-range blood alcohol reading of 0.145.

A few friends had dropped in, including Ally. Sometime after ten o'clock, Christopher and Ally fought and she went home with her mother. Christopher left Jack's house without saying goodbye. At about 10:25, Jack went to look for him and noticed his car was gone. He sent Ally a text message asking if Christopher was with her.

She replied, 'No, why?'

'Because he's left my house and I don't know where he is. I'm worried.'

Shortly after, Christopher's close friend Emma messaged Ally: 'I'm so worried about Chris. He's at south Avalon headland and he's talking about suicide.'

Ally relayed this to Jack. Jack then messaged Christopher.

Taken from police statements:

AUGUST 29TH, 2002. 10:30 P.M.
'Where are you?' Jack's message read.

'At Avalon headland. It's good to know you care. Love you bro,' Christopher messaged back. And then Christopher's phone went dead. Panicked, Jack rode his bike from his house down the hill to the beach headland a kilometre away.

10:40 P.M.
A frightened Ally ran up to the main house to get her mother and sister. They drove together to the headland.

Jack arrived at the beach and saw Christopher's car facing east with all four doors wide open and the keys in the ignition. But he couldn't find Christopher. A few minutes later, Jack saw him walking back from the base of the cliff to the grassed area near the top of the precipice. He ran to him.

'Don't ever do that to me again,' Jack said. 'You scared me. I love you, mate.'

He hugged Christopher who was 'agitated and highly distressed'. They walked to his car. Christopher hit the passenger side external mirror with his arm then threw it off the cliff.

'I kept asking him what was wrong but he just kept saying "nothing",' Jack stated.

Then Ally and her family joined them. Her mother and sister were told to wait in the car while Ally went to Christopher.

'He was crying and distressed,' she stated. 'I hugged him.'

Ally recalled that Christopher kept repeating: 'I hate everything.'

'I don't think you understand how many people love you and look up to you,' she told him.

He then said he had to find his phone and started to walk down the hill. Ally asked Jack what had happened to his phone.

'He threw it off the cliff instead of himself,' Jack told her.

10:45 P.M.
Jack got a torch out of Christopher's car to go and look for the mirror.

11–11:20 P.M.
While Jack continued to look for the mirror, Christopher and Ally walked down the hill to the picnic tables. They were joined by Ally's mother and sister and shortly after by Jack. Ally then told her mother and sister to go home, which they did. Christopher gave Ally his phone which was missing the keypad and the back cover. She turned it on and received a message but couldn't read it because the front cover was missing. She put his SIM card into her phone to read the message.

I never found out who the message was from or what it said.

Ally asked him if he wanted to talk about how he felt. He said, 'It's unexplainable, no one will ever understand.'

She said she and Jack were hugging him when Christopher suddenly decided to go and look for the missing parts of his phone. He walked off by himself down to the bottom of the headland with the torch.

'We weren't worried about him because we were at the bottom of the headland and he had calmed down heaps,' she stated.

11:25 P.M.
Christopher had been gone for five minutes when Jack and Ally decided to check on him.

Ally: 'We walked down the edge of the beach towards the swimming pool. Above the pool, about two-thirds of the way up the cliff, I saw the torch moving and I could also see the outline of Chris climbing upwards. We were on the pool side of the fence and I yelled out, "Chris, what are you doing?" He kept climbing.'

Jack: 'I couldn't really see Chris, just the movement of the torch. I yelled out his name then looked at Ally.'

11:30 P.M.

Jack: 'As I looked up I saw Chris falling from the top of the cliff and it looked like his body rolled a couple of times as he was coming down. I saw him land right in front of us but on the opposite side of the fence. We ran around and I called 000 for an ambulance. I also called Chris's parents. When I got there he was already unconscious and he was lying on the rocks on his back facing upwards. I could see some blood on his face and also a pool of blood under his head.'

Ally: 'All of a sudden I saw Chris falling backwards off the cliff. I think part of him hit the cliff on the way down. He landed directly in front of where we were standing behind the fence. As I ran around to the other side I dialled 000. Jack called Chris's parents. I told Jack to give me his jumper and I placed it under Chris's head. I saw that he had blood running from his ears, mouth and head. I called my mum and said, "Get down here, Chris has fallen."

'I grabbed his hand and said, "If you can hear me, squeeze my hand", but there was no movement. I placed my cheek against his mouth and could feel a slight breath.'

The ambulance officers arrived then, followed shortly by Phil and I, and Christopher was carried to the ambulance. While

Phil and I waited outside the ambulance doors, Jack, Ally and her family were about 25 metres away as they told police their version of events. When the ambulance drove away Ally and Jack went to the hospital. The ambulance doors were open; they saw Christopher lying in the back with a sheet covering his body, his feet 'hanging out'. It was then they knew Christopher had 'passed away'.

Both Jack and Ally stated they were unsure whether he jumped or fell.

Ally's final statement reads: 'All I can say is that when he fell, there was the sound of rocks falling but no screams from him.'

From the statement of the ambulance officer, Terry:

11:45 P.M.
'When I got to the patient his body was partly lying in water which was discoloured red with blood. He had an amount of bleeding from his mouth. I found him unconscious with multiple lower limb fractures, a very faint carotid pulse and no sign of respiration. There were obvious signs of injury to his upper body. His pupils were fixed and dilated.'

The two officers rolled Christopher onto a spinal board and along with two other officers from an intensive care ambulance commenced CPR. He was intubated.

'Heavy bleeding continued through the tube and it became evident that the patient had massive internal injuries,' Terry stated. 'These injuries were incompatible with life and the patient was pronounced deceased at midnight.'

Jack eventually found the mirror—a metre away from where Christopher's body landed. Ally would find the rest of his phone. By the time I got it back from police weeks later, all his messages had been wiped.

Christopher loved Bunny, his Buddha, incense and moonstones. He hated injustice, cruelty, judgement.

He was scared of the dark and being alone.

That's how he died.

He didn't even scream.

chapter 18

As I write this, the last leaf of the weeping birch flutters onto the murky surface of the sandstone birdbath. It sits among the forget-me-nots in an arched garden I created when we first moved here three years ago. A red climbing rose, shadowed by a large crab apple, struggles over one arch and on the other, a pink and a white clematis hold hands for the cold months ahead. The grape hyacinths and jonquils have popped through their mulched blanket and when I scratch just below the surface, the tips of hundreds of orange, yellow and white daffodils hint an annual promise of a carpet of wintry cheer. The black tulips, bluebells and the purple-veined crocus will be next, completing the coloured splendour in a leafless winter garden.

In a corner near the fish pond, a semi-naked Chinese elm quivers. My favourite tree—I've planted one in every garden I've owned. Although this one is only 3 metres tall, in time its crown will match the 20-metre sycamore.

My Chinese elm started out as a 3-centimetre sapling in a pot which Daisy gave to me during our years of renting. He had taken it as a cutting from Christopher's memorial tree which was planted at Shore's preparatory school and rugby grounds at Northbridge a month after he died. Only 3 metres tall at the time, the memorial tree is now a 15-metre majestic grandfather, shading the playground's forecourt and tall enough to be seen from the rugby oval. It was commissioned by Headmaster Grant who, in his final year at Shore, wanted to leave a legacy for our son. He had chosen a Chinese elm, unaware it was my favourite tree.

At its base a plaque, mounted on a large rock, reads:

Christopher Newling 'Cricket' 22.10.1984–29.8.2002.
At Shore 1996–2002.
Vitai Lampada Traditit; He Handed On The Torch Of Life.

Recently, Phil and I went to see the tree for the first time since it was planted. We had avoided the rugby grounds, the memories too sad. Kelly Courtnall is a teacher at the prep school's early learning centre, and she arranged for us to visit the tree during school hours. She was also a great friend of Christopher's.

I was worried I wouldn't recognise her but when she put her arms around us and smiled, it was as if no time had passed. As we entered the playground, a throng of five- and six-year-olds gathered around her, calling out her name: 'Hello, Miss Kelly!' She is strikingly beautiful with long, straight blonde hair framing a delicate face with porcelain skin. But it was her warmth and kindness which attracted us as we talked under the wide limbs of Christopher's tree.

'He was a very good friend to me,' she says. 'When I was sixteen, I had a stroke and was in hospital, rehab and then at home for quite a long time. Chris was home, too, after his leg operations. He came over every day for a while to sit with me. We talked and watched movies together. It was such a special time.'

Kelly says Christopher was a supportive friend who shared with her their common stories of struggle. She says she never knew he was depressed.

'He always seemed so full of love, laughter and light-hearted fun. He was the life of the party—the popular one. He was so easy to love. I heard from others he was having a hard time but I presumed it would pass.

'I started teaching at Shore three years ago. I noticed the tree and the plaque on my first day teaching here. I didn't know it was Chris's tree. It shocked me when I read the plaque. I sat here and cried and cried.'

Now she says she loves looking at the tree, watching the children play around and in it. When the kids ask her to read the plaque, they always say, 'Who's Cricket?'

She tells them he used to play rugby here and was a very special friend.

chapter 19

~

I didn't know her name. She was someone's daughter, someone's mother, maybe someone's wife. But she was alone, alone with her grief, her particular madness. She draped herself over the handrail at the top of the stairs near the entrance of one of Sydney's major psychiatric hospitals in a leafy suburb on the North Shore. It was early afternoon but her hair was mussed as if she'd just woken and didn't care. She wore a grey tracksuit which sagged at the knees and well-worn ugg boots, stained with ash and egg yolk. A cigarette dangled from her dry and cracked lips. She drew back, exhaled then coughed with a guttural explosion. She glared at Phil and me as we hesitated on the first step. She thought I was 'going in' by the wild look in my eye and by the way Phil was steering me with a gentle hand at my elbow.

The corridor was long and narrow. The white walls had yellowed over the years and were stamped like a child's painting with handprints. Doors to the wards were all open and men and women stared at us as we walked slowly past. I smiled at them but they didn't return my phoney bonhomie. They all had lost interest some time ago. The stench of chlorine and urine wafted after us as we shuffled discreetly down the hall. Somewhere nearby a woman screamed, a wail so mournful I wanted to go to her. Phil grabbed my hand and forced me to keep up with him until we reached the glassed, bulletproof, locked cubicle at the end of the hall. Nic was in there. They had locked up our sixteen-year-old because he wanted to die just like his brother did two months before. He was in a room just big enough for a single bed and a chair. He was asleep, his cordless computer opened by his feet, his school uniform slung over his bag in the corner of the ward.

His school counsellor, John Burns, and Gordon Parker had agreed Nic wasn't coping at school. John had called me that morning for my permission to admit him. I knew it was serious because, even though I said I'd pick Nic up from school, John said he'd take him as the hospital was just five minutes away.

I ran my fingers through Nic's hair and kissed his bloated cheek. He stirred, opened his eyes, then closed them again. He didn't want to see us. He didn't want to talk about why he was there. He just was and we had to accept it. And somehow we had to live with the horror that we may lose another child.

My mother was in this hospital five years before but two floors down on the drug and alcohol ward, one floor above the eating disorder unit. She nearly died, too. My father was overseas and she didn't want to live either. She drank herself into a stupor and fell down the stairs at home. A neighbour found her, called me and I drove her bruised and battered body into this hospital. Doctors knocked her out with Valium. I sat crying by her bedside all night while Phil looked after our boys. The doctor told me to get help, because, he said matter-of-factly, children of alcoholics need support, too. I wondered what he would say if he saw me now, sitting by Nic who wanted to die to finally free himself of the demons in his head and because that's what his brother did eight weeks earlier.

Over the following days his depression gave way to his mania. He was allowed his computer cord but only under supervision. He spent every waking minute designing T-shirts of 'Criddy', funny ones which captured his smile, his naughty personality. Nic turned him into an animated cricket, standing, ankles crossed against a lamp post, smoking a cigarette.

He asked a friend to help him with the design and manufacture, and every day there was a new T-shirt, a new cricket with something else to say.

He'd ask us what we thought and we encouraged him, anything to keep him focused and alive. He was exhausting—talking too fast to be understood, swiping at the keyboard in hurried jabs too quick for the eye to follow.

The nurses told us they had to take the computer away from him at night so he would get some rest but by morning's light he would be at it again, only breaking for something to eat.

We were told he'd be in the hospital for at least ten days. Gordon, who had no jurisdiction at this hospital, still came to see him every day. He called us after one visit to tell us he thought he'd finally diagnosed Nic. For the first time he had witnessed Nic's mania. He was almost certain Nic had bipolar disorder, which necessitated a whole new set of medications.

After a week it was deemed he was safe enough to be moved into a non-acute ward. Unbeknown to Phil and me at the time, he was put into a ward with three other men, all in their forties. That night while Phil and I sat silently on the deck I felt a jab of panic in my chest. Something was wrong. I couldn't get my breath and my lungs were screaming. Phil poured me a strong drink and I drained it. He put his arms around me until my panic eased.

'Something is wrong,' I said to him breathlessly. 'I have to ring Nic.'

His phone rang and rang until he finally answered. He sounded strange. He told me he had been moved from the acute ward. I heard the fear in his voice.

'Are you okay, Nic?'

Silence.

'Nic! Are you okay?'

Silence, although I was sure I heard him crying.

'What's wrong, Nic?'

'Nothing.'

'I'm coming in.'

'No, don't, Mum. I'm okay.'

His voice was flat, uninterested, monotonic.

'I'm worried about you, Nic.'

He couldn't talk. I could hear the emotion in his breathing, the sharp intake of air. I knew for certain he was crying.

'I'm leaving now, Nic.'

'No, Mum! I'm sorry, Mum. I just can't do this anymore. I'm so sorry, Mum. Forgive me, Mum.'

'No, Nic, no! Please. Please wait for us. Please, we're coming now. Please, Nic.'

The phone went dead.

Hearing my end of the conversation and my panic, Phil had called Daisy, who screeched up the driveway as I called Gordon at home. I told him that Nic was alone and going to kill himself. I was hysterical, screaming. He told me he'd ring me back after he spoke to his colleague, the psychiatrist looking after Nic.

Daisy broke all records getting to the hospital so it only took us half an hour.

Gordon called back. The off-duty psychiatrist had alerted staff and was on his way to the hospital. Gordon and I talked continually during the trip as updates came through. We knew they had found him, we knew he was alive, but nothing else.

Daisy, Phil and I ran into the hospital, not caring about the noise or who we crashed into. A nurse tried to slow me, calm me, but I told her to fuck off. A doctor led us into a quiet anteroom where Nic was lying on a high examination bed. He looked dead.

I reassured myself with an ear to his mouth. He had been heavily sedated and his wrists were bandaged. I laid my head down on his chest and sobbed. After an hour, Phil and Daisy wanted to take me home but I wouldn't leave until the psychiatrist assured me Nic wouldn't wake till morning and would be closely monitored. 'Like before?' I wanted to say, but what would that have achieved?

The next day Nic was back in the lock-up ward. He was lying like a toddler, his head under the sheets.

I lifted a corner and was shocked to see how pale and sad he looked, even with his eyes closed.

'I love you,' I whispered in his ear.

He opened his eyes and smiled wanly.

'Me too,' he managed.

I wanted to ask him why he wanted to die but I already knew. Tears leaked through the slits in his fingers and he sobbed, giving in to his devastation.

I nearly lost him. How could I protect him when I couldn't

save Christopher? How could I battle and beat the monsters who chant 'be dead' in his head? How could I swaddle him in a blanket of maternal cottonwool when I couldn't promise him I'd be there to catch him? As his mother, how could I allow myself to fail again?

It felt like a test—a trial of redemption which I knew I didn't have the courage or the strength to perform. Then I looked into his eyes, so empty, so desperate, and realised I was his only chance. But what hope could I offer when I didn't want to live, either. Ironically, he would end up being my only chance, a second chance to save a son.

'I love you, Nic.'

He tried to smile, then closed his eyes. I stroked his hair and held his hand tightly.

'I'll always love you, no matter what. Remember that,' I said.

He opened his eyes. They were lifeless, dark pools in a bottomless pit. Fresh tears fell, a waterfall to the pillow under his head. He reached out and pulled me to him.

'I need you, Mum.'

For Nic

Sometimes, when I chance a look at my son
I can see the pain behind the smear of his veneer
He will catch me—sometimes
I move my mood
Smile
Try to make amends
Too late
I ask him how he is

He shuffles
He knows me too well
He tries to filter through the quagmire of his mind
Accessing only the immediate
The rest swirls and twirls in a murky maelstrom of confusion.
He rocks from side to side
If I die, you couldn't live in this house
You'd see me in every room
You'd hear me laugh—my violin

I'd hear him cry.

How could I?

How could I stand in this room

Where he spent days crafting a shield for King Arthur

The room where he laughed along with Johnny Bravo

His bedroom where a thousand words are locked

In cellular time capsules

Where his boyhood clown has been left to rest for the day

If I don't live . . .

He falls silent

He can't bear to see me cry

But he doesn't need to explain

I know him too well.

chapter 20

Nic came home a few weeks later, just before Christmas. He didn't want to; he was scared. He didn't trust himself or me. The shine in his eyes had dulled and his heavy step shuffled with dread through our unhappy home. He was grey and spiritless, indistinct as though sheathed in plastic wrap. He didn't want to eat, drink or talk.

'Too tired,' he said, pulling Clowny out of his bag. 'Maybe later.'

Night had finally fallen on this dark day. Phil and I waited, watched and listened as Nic slept. We tried to wake him to eat but he had no desire.

I should have been grateful my son was down the hall, asleep, and I didn't understand why I wasn't.

'Fear,' Phil said.

Yes. Fear is as powerful as grief is poisonous. It permeates the skin, seeps into the blood and winds a soporific venal path into the already burdened heart. It smells like turned fish, the pungent odour leaking out through every pore. Fear makes you sick. It mutates into a mass in the pit of your gut where it beats and pulsates then releases the bile in a spasm that renders you breathless.

The next day was long and agonising as I watched Nic sleep the hours away. I wondered what he had prayed for. Did he ask the God he believed in to help him live or did he secretly still want to die so he could be with Criddy?

~

Phil and I pretended to be good parents while shuffling past each other like invalids; like mutes we nodded at unnecessary questions. We were drained and desperate, cold and intractable. We had been stunned by shock; electrical jolts had cauterised our nerves which dangled flaccidly in an airless lacuna.

Although Nic was still alive, it felt like death to me.

We spent the following days stroking and soothing him, pulling him out of bed and back into life. After a few weeks I began to see a glimmer of my former son. Phil made him laugh, I made him eat. His smile slowly returned along with the light in his sky-blue eyes. He told jokes again, laughed, loved, lived. He still slept most of the day and night as his body and mind adjusted to the new medication and although panic punched my heart with predictable beats, there were times I heard myself breathe. Gordon was pleased with his recovery and that the drug-resistant Nic was finally properly diagnosed and medicated.

Nic loved Christmas. Knowing I wouldn't be able to celebrate it, Phil decided to take him to America. They had a white Christmas in Colorado with Bill, a friend of my brother Tom, then went to Disney World in Florida. Phil said Nic was still very unwell but being away from home made him happy. Nic wanted me to go with them and Phil was wary of leaving me on my own that first year.

But I couldn't. How could I tell them I had to stay back for Christopher? By some miracle I didn't quite understand yet, Christopher could still come home. I sat on the deck each night, watching the top of the driveway just in case, and for years to come I would refuse to travel or venture far from home. Phil went overseas three times, twice with Nic.

Nic returned to school at the start of the next year, 2003. Although he tried to fit back in, he struggled with his tiredness and 'fuzzy' brain. One teacher berated him because he fell asleep on his desk, despite school counsellor John Burns' order to allow Nic to go at his own pace. I knew he also missed his brothers and Christopher's mates who had graduated the year before. Ben was in his second year studying music at Newcastle University.

After a few months and on advice from John and Headmaster Grant, it was decided Nic could no longer continue his high school education.

He was never going to be a vet, a lawyer or famous violinist. Suddenly, he had nowhere to go, nothing to do. He filled his days with computer games and comedy shows on television.

We kept a vigilant eye on him but as the weeks turned into months he became more animated and confident and we tried to give him breathing space. He knew he couldn't go back to school so he taught himself the intricacies of computers, their design and technology. He spent hours every day scouring IT websites. He'd find broken computers, take them apart, then rebuild them.

We had a long way to go. The effort of watching Nic, being a mother and a wife when all I wanted was to sleep, was starting to rankle me. I felt like a pawn in Nic's world, beholden to his moods. Resentment and ennui were layering as I was forced to listen to Nic's monologues and to endure Phil's silences. I couldn't escape and if I did I was pulled back into Nic's world. Tension built and demands pricked like insults. I didn't want to be here but I had nowhere else to go.

chapter 21

~

A daddy-long-leg spider has spent the night under the lip of my printer. As I fire it up for the day to write, it stretches its back, unfurls its legs and scurries on an invisible thread to the rose-etched cornice.

Outside my study window in Leura in the Blue Mountains, thunder rumbles behind the tall pine trees. Suddenly, after two dry months, the heavens finally weep; the tiny white pebbles in Christopher's garden jump like popcorn. Hooded and warm I go to sit among the bustle. I grab handfuls of pebbles then let them slip through the gullies of my cold fingers. Christopher's concrete sentinels—bunny, wombat and the weeping Buddha—turn to slate as the rain soaks and spills and runs in tributaries down their spines. Somewhere over the range, close and high, lightning cracks, splitting the gunmetal sky in two. I jump.

When I was a child, lightning meant God was angry. His electric finger always pointed at me and I knew I'd done something very wrong. But then I grew up and a storm was just a storm which frightened me.

As a child, lightning frightened Ben, too. Thunder made him run to my arms and when the jagged cracks rattled a window, he'd bury his head under my shirt.

When he was a baby, he cried almost all the time. No one knew why. Maybe his brain hurt; maybe tiny seizures were giving him headaches. He was four when he had his first epileptic fit. He had many more and was eventually given Epilim, an anticonvulsive drug.

His crying decreased when he started to walk at eight months. He became master of his little body. He was a quiet, loving, gentle toddler who never got into trouble.

We wrestled, painted and made mud pies for the goblins hiding under the cubby house. We sang, read stories and made up silly rhymes. I was in love with him. I had never known that love before, the aching, constant need to touch, kiss, hold. He became my reason for everything.

When Ben was born my brother Jim bought him a toy carousel. Its hood was striped with red and blue and when the key was turned, four delicate horses rose and lowered on a yellow totem pole. A lullaby played a slow, melodic carnival tune which stilled our little boy every night at bedtime. Then Jim died and Ben couldn't understand why I didn't want to hear the lullaby anymore.

It was a rainy, early summer morning when a truck turned left and Jim, on his motorbike, skidded into the back of it. I was visiting my mother, Ben on my hip, when my father tore up the driveway, his face a tortured mask. In the following days my father raged and my mother shrank further into her psyche. She started to drink again. We didn't have a funeral; my parents were too distressed. The crematorium wasn't expecting my older brother and sister and I as we placed flowers on Jim's coffin minutes before he disappeared behind the black velvet curtain. My father wanted his ashes buried under a tree in bushland not far from my parents' house. He bought a tree and we all traipsed down a track and then through dense bushland.

I went several times to the makeshift memorial but then the tree died and I couldn't find the site.

~

Before Jim died, death was someone else's misery. I didn't know death and I gave it no thought. Other people lost their mothers, fathers, brothers, sisters, sons and daughters. I didn't. After Jim died I was scared of it but only in the way that it cut me in half.

As horrifying and painful as it was, I found some solace in that I now had my loss, my one death, and it couldn't happen again.

Death was now my misery. It wrapped itself around me like a pungent ether. It nudged me when I smiled. I closed my lips over my teeth to keep it from seeping inside of me but it still hovered around my senses like fermenting food. The chasm between life and death—a narrow gully without a safety net.

Born only eighteen months apart, Jim and I were very close. After returning from the crematorium I held Ben tightly while he slept. I closed my eyes and imagined a world without this beautiful, healthy son. My parents had four children, Phil and I only one.

Christopher James was born ten months later. He had blond hair and bright blue eyes. He was beautiful. If I had believed in God or the spiritual world and reincarnation, I would have hoped my gentle, loving brother had resumed his life in the soul of my new baby. I looked for signs but after a while I stopped searching for Jim in Christopher's eyes.

When Nic entered the world twenty-one months later, Ben became the family's lieutenant, taking the role of father when Phil was away. He told Christopher not to climb too high, Nic not to spin too fast. He let them have the biggest piece of cake. He was proud of them. When Christopher was the first one to ride a bike, Ben patted him on the back like a chuffed dad. When Nic beat them both at a spelling test, Ben told him he was smart. We encouraged their friendships, wanting them to always have a strong fraternal bond.

But when they grew apart in adolescence, when Nic became manic and Christopher was running wild, Ben lost his authority. He had suffered his own depression and was already weakened when the unknown and sinister force invaded Nic's head; he was dazed by the fun-loving, sporty Christopher who became a stranger by his own demons.

They all saw themselves in each other during their individual periods of illness. Christopher and Ben were scared of Nic's mania, walking around him nervously. Nic wanted to be in their circle of friends, anything to appear normal. Ben stood by silently as he witnessed the strain on Phil and me, as we struggled to keep Christopher out of trouble, at the same time scared to death of losing Nic.

～

When Phil and Nic were in America in 2003, Ben and I had a rare night together. It was a warm January evening and we stood on the deck, throwing meat to the kookaburras and butcher birds.

'How are you, Ben?'

'Good,' he said as he pulled the top off his beer.

'Really?'

I looked at him deeply. He looked down, knowing his answer wouldn't satisfy me.

'You have to get it out, Ben.'

He breathed in deeply as one tear fell matched by another bulging in the acute angle of his eye. His chest heaved and he swayed on unsteady legs as he took another sip. He sat down next to me and I grabbed his free hand.

'Talk to me, Ben.'

'I can't, Mum.'

But the sadness was there, etched in his brow, his stormy eyes and at the commas of his downturned lips. He hated what Christopher's death had done to our family, how we had been serrated into individual entities, our souls silenced into stones.

'How are you, Mum?'

'It's hard.'

'I know.'

I nodded because he did know and I knew I could never take his pain away. He was only nineteen. Like me, he would never get over losing his brother.

He would always wonder what Christopher would have become. Would they have sailed together, gone to the pub, taken their kids on holidays together? Would they have become friends? Grief prevented Ben from continuing with his music degree. He came home and eventually moved into a flat with Sarah, who loved and nurtured him. He found a job marketing a Sydney basketball team. During the season, and without him knowing, he was being watched by one of the supporters, the head of a leading bank, who offered him a job.

Ben drained his beer and stood up in front of me. He hugged me hard; his intensity squeezed my heart.

'I love you, Mum.'

I felt his tears run down the back of my neck and I buried my face into his shoulder. He cleared his throat then released me.

I watched the slump of his slow stride, the sorrow and defeat in the way he held his head. I couldn't help but feel guilty.

When Ben cries, his face contorts, reddens and folds in on itself as he fights against it. He doesn't like to cry; he is strong, the big brother, protector. He cried when Christopher died and a year later when his beloved Shadow was diagnosed with cancer.

I know Ben cries at other times—when he's alone. Perhaps on his one-man skiff out on Sydney Harbour. Drenched by the waves, no one would ever know if the vertical streaks which stain his tanned face are slashes from the sea or salt-encrusted tears.

From too much love of living
From hope and fear set free,
We thank with brief thanksgiving
Whatever gods may be
That no life lives forever
That dead men rise up never;
That even the weariest river
Winds somewhere safe to sea

ALGERNON SWINBURNE, FROM 'HEALING AFTER THE SUICIDE OF A LOVED ONE'

chapter 22

~

AUGUST 29TH, 2003

The heavens and stars were invisible above a thick canopy of black clouds as we all gathered at the headland for the first anniversary. The full moon, the night's sleepy eye, winked an intermittent glow. Ben and I, Daisy and his wife Mandy, Trish, my close friend and Murgy's mother, and a large group of Christopher's friends and rugby mates stood underneath the floodlight near the edge of the precipice. The cliff face and the pool below looked like an eerie moonscape under the harsh, fluorescent glow. The only sound was the crashing of the waves and a distant car horn. We were quiet for a long time. Troy, a rugby mate who read the eulogy at the memorial service on behalf of Christopher's friends, filled our glasses with wine then we raised them to make a toast to Christopher, Chris, Cricket, Criddy, Crick, Newls. We sat down and held on to the person next to us. Silent sobs and whispered regrets filled the air on that cold and wind-free night. The silence was broken as Troy played Christopher's favourite song on his car's stereo, a signal to stand, all of us clutching our single-stemmed red roses. We raised them and in one quick motion, threw them over the cliff. With a loud crack, the floodlight snapped shut, whipping the light back into its domed head. I heard a collective gasp.

Not wanting to leave us on our own—Phil and Nic were in Ireland—everyone piled into cars and went back to our place. We drank more wine, talked and reminisced then fell asleep where we sat.

AUGUST 29TH, 2004

A full moon danced on the horizon's brim, unsettling the midnight blue ocean which shimmied under its spotlight. The night air bristled across our skins as we sought refuge in each other's touch. Nic put his arm around me in the car park outside our favourite restaurant in Avalon across the road from the beach. There was a faint smell of garbage mingled with sea spray from a gathering southerly. Departing diners gave us a cursory glance before diving into the warmth of their cars. Nic suddenly let go of me, raised his gym-booted foot and crunched the life out of a scurrying cockroach. Yellow pus oozed out of the flattened insect. He giggled. I groaned.

Phil, Ben, Nic and I walked across the road to the headland and were joined by last year's group. I was so grateful they were there, that they still remembered their friend. Ben and Phil walked away to a private place to stand in silence. Nic and I sat down together, our bodies touching in the frigid air. I laid my head on his shoulder. We were silent for the longest time.

Then Nic cleared his throat and whispered something but his words fell away, taken by the eddying breeze and thrown to the crashing waves below. The irony knocked the wind out of me. I gulped, releasing a tiny whine. Nic leaned in closer and tried again.

'Criddy sacrificed his life for me.'

I hugged him tight and shook my head furiously.

'He did, Mum. I didn't know until the next morning what happened but that night I was suicidal. I wanted to die, too. I rang Kids Helpline. A woman talked to me for hours. I didn't know you and Dad weren't home. I didn't know you were here with Criddy.'

I felt the familiar rip in my heart.

'Is that why you're still alive?' I whispered.

He nodded sadly and pulled at a tuft of grass. I heard his quiet sobs.

Other friends arrived, gathering in a group under the floodlight. I was glad Nic and I were at the other side of the verge, in a quiet, dark corner. His body quivered as he quietly explained.

'I think Criddy wanted me to live. It was always going to be me or him. You knew that, right?'

I wiped my nose across my jacket sleeve and breathed in deeply. I shook my head. I couldn't bear to confess I had no idea Christopher wanted to die.

'You don't want to live either, do you?'

'No. Not really, Nic.'

'Why, Mum?'

'I failed. I couldn't save Christopher and I'm probably going to lose you, too.'

'But you saved me.'

I threw my head in my hands and sobbed. The group came over and we were both lifted by strong arms.

'And I'll save you,' Nic added.

'You're taking away my choices,' I whispered in his ear.

'And all mine have been taken from me.'

I understood then what he meant. Nic felt Christopher's sacrifice had to be honoured and in turn I had to honour him.

Flowers were handed out and once again we stood in silent prayer on what would become an annual ritual. We raised them in harmony and threw them in the air.

Dozens of red roses, like rubies on a black cape, dotted the sky before falling to the rocks below. Then the floodlight went out with an audible whoosh. Nic found my hand in the dark as we walked back to the car park. He led me to a spot under a streetlight and took off his jacket. He lifted the tattered sleeve of his T-shirt. On his left bicep was a tattoo, still raw and raised from the day before's needle. A red heart, about 10 centimetres in diameter, was surrounded by red rosebuds and in the middle, a small trail of ivy wound around a word in dark, black ink—'MUM'.

He smiled at me proudly. I shook my head with disbelief.

'That's there forever,' I admonished.

'Precisely.'

Several weeks after Christopher died, his friend Sam tattooed 'NEWLS' on his lower back in big, bold letters. Phil saw it when Sam's T-shirt lifted while he was slam-dunking a basketball. Murgy tattooed NEWLS on the left side of his chest. Our nephew Dan, who was very close to Christopher but living in America, had his initials, CJN, tattooed on the inside of his arm. That's all there was. Inked memories of what could have been.

AUGUST 29TH, 2005

The quarter moon hung in the eastern sky like a hammock, affording a minimal glow on the dark horizon. The waves crashed on the rocks below.

I had been sick for days in anticipation of reliving another anniversary. Three years. I clutched a handful of roses as we made our way up to the windy headland. It was cold as it always was at the end of August. We climbed over the white fence and sat cross-legged on the grass.

Ben filled our plastic glasses with red wine as we huddled together in silence. We were all deep in our private thoughts, the floodlight casting an eerie pall on this sad gathering.

A car arrived, lighting up our backs. Four of Christopher's friends, whom I hadn't seen since his death, jumped out and climbed over the railing to hug me. I gave them each a rose as we stood to throw them to the wind.

The floodlight died. I heard the intake of breath behind me as some of the boys witnessed for the first time the phenomenon others had already seen. Annabel gripped me tightly. Trish put her arm around my neck; I could hear her smiling knowingly.

After a while we got up to go home. Troy put his strong arms around my waist and hoisted me over the fence before helping Trish and the other girls. He's always been a gentleman.

'It happens every year?' one of the boys whispered to me. 'The floodlight?'

I nodded. His eyes were wide and there was a tremor in his voice. I knew he'd come back the next night on his own.

Murgy was studying at Charles Sturt University in Bathurst but rang me on every anniversary when he couldn't be there. We shared a warm and childish friendship since he and Christopher became best mates in their first year in high school. Murgy is as charismatic, naughty, athletic and beguiling as Christopher was. Often they'd compete on the rugby field and with girlfriends but they always remained close. Trish and I became best friends through the deep relationship our sons shared. Together, Trish and I were as naughty as they were and they'd often laugh at our antics.

missing christopher

~

Being private-school mothers and living on Sydney's Northern Beaches, we tried our hardest to fit in with the North Shore mothers who dressed well, spoke clearly and were *au fait* with protocol. Trish and I bumbled our way through school functions, laughing at each other when we put a step wrong. As mothers of boys in the rugby First Fifteen, we were obliged to bring a plate of food for afternoon tea at the home games. On the first occasion, Trish and I met in the clubhouse where a long table, draped in white linen, was adorned with china plates and tiered cake stands. Our paper plates were covered with foil. I lifted the edge of her foil and cackled loudly. She had picked up a bun from the local bakery; the icing had stuck to the foil. She ripped at my foil revealing a pile of burnt sausage rolls and party pies. We were laughing so hard we feared we'd be caught as we quickly hid our plates among the cucumber and dill sandwiches, the salmon and avocado dips and homemade sushi rolls all on Royal Doulton platters (we checked).

'I know the sausage rolls are yours,' Murgy whispered in my ear.

I smiled and kissed him on the cheek as Christopher laid a heavy, sweaty arm around Trish's shoulder. She shook a finger at him and scolded, 'Don't you dare.'

~

Murgy and I share the same birthday and have an annual competition to see who can be first to phone the other to mark the occasion. Nicola, his older sister by a few years, had a close relationship with Christopher but saw little of him during the last year, as he sank deeper into his depression.

Just after the second anniversary of Christopher's death, she had just returned from a trip to Brazil. She sounded agitated when she called to ask me to meet her in Avalon for dinner. She had something very important to tell me.

It would take me several years to begin to grasp her story. Over that time I had to ask her to repeat its details and then finally to write it down so I could understand the consequences of an experience which deeply disturbed her.

She wrote in a letter to me: 'I will never forget what happened to me in Brazil and even though I didn't see Chris much in the last year, I have always felt a connection to him, and still do. During 2004 I went to Brazil with a few close friends including Kristy, a Brazilian girl whom I didn't know very well. Within the first few weeks of our trip, I got to know her better and discovered she had a sensitivity for spiritual energy. We were in the old city of Salvador in the state of Bahia. We stayed in a very old and historic townhouse in a back street of the city. One night, we were getting ready to go out when we heard Kristy screaming in the bathroom. We rushed in. She said someone had appeared in the mirror. As we were trying to comfort her she asked if any one of us knew a man who had passed away. I wasn't thinking of Chris as I didn't think it could be related.

'Kristy said the apparition had said to her "Trisha, Ben, Nicola". I thought then it had to be Chris. Kristy didn't know my mother's name. I asked her to describe him; she said she couldn't see his face as he had a red cap pulled down over his eyes. [Christopher always wore a red cap—always pulled down over his face.] Kristy said he told her that he had thought by killing himself he could stop his pain and that he didn't realise how much it would affect everyone close to him as he believed no one would really care if he was alive or not. He also said he really regrets what he did. He told Kristy that everyone must let go of him because he couldn't move on.'

Nicola sent me a photograph of Kristy who was working as a fashion designer in Bali. She is a petite and beautiful woman with piercing brown eyes, dark hair and olive skin. Nicola says she is a friendly, open, generous person but, beneath the surface, a little fragile. She told Nicola during their two-month holiday that her spirituality deeply troubled her as she felt burdened by the suffering of others, especially in the spiritual sense. Her gift was her millstone as she didn't want to be the bridge between worlds which brought spirits to her in search of help. She never encouraged it and still doesn't, hoping this connection will one day subside. Nicola says Kristy was 'freaked out' when she saw the apparition in the mirror because she was caught unprepared.

When Nicola realised it had to be Christopher, she was very sad as she knew how depressed and despondent he had felt leading up to his death and that from his other world he was witnessing the devastation he left behind.

'I also felt happy that I had the chance to reconnect with him and it left me feeling that he must be around all the time, close to us, and we are just not aware of his presence,' Nicola wrote. 'I also knew that in some way, he was asking me to speak to you, I suppose in the hope it would bring you some peace and allow him to move on. When I got home to Australia, I had an overwhelming feeling that I had to tell both you and my brother what had happened. It was very hard for me, as it was all very strange and I knew how my story would be received, that is, with disbelief or that I had gone mad.'

My friend Deby, whose son Laurie was born on the same day and at the same hospital as Christopher, told me about her experience. Our sons had grown up together until Deby moved to Queensland after the death to cancer of her husband Steve and when the boys were in their early teens. She said that a week before Christopher died, she had bought me a card but hadn't got around to sending it. On the day he died she picked it up to post it and found a dead cricket near the stamp. She flicked it off and it fell behind her chest of drawers.

Deby later told me: 'On the night it happened, Yaina [Deby's daughter] and I were at a friend's house. At 11:15 a strange feeling came over me. I was very unsettled and Yaina could see how agitated I was. I pretended I wasn't feeling well and we went home. I couldn't sleep all night.'

A few days after the funeral, Deby bought me a sundial for Christopher's garden because 'time is important'.

After she got home she found the dead cricket and buried it under a birdbath I had given her years before.

The sundial is now in my Blue Mountains garden, next to the Chinese elm.

Do not cheat thy Heart and tell her grief will pass away.

ADELAIDE PROCTER

chapter 23

The sand was cold and wet between my toes and the wind skated across the waves, hitting my skin with a slap. The palm trees were bent like bananas. It was the day after the third anniversary. The beach was empty except for a lone jogger who circled around me on each lap. An oil tanker on the horizon looked like a bath toy as it crept south to Botany Bay.

It was a grey, depressing day. As I buried my feet in the sand I wondered why, after three years, my grief was heavier than ever?

No one warned me how lonely grief would be. I became a stranger to those who loved me and for others, I was the missing piece in the jigsaw puzzle they'd already solved. I feared them for what they may say and how they would judge.

'Are you over it yet?' one acquaintance said to Phil when he bumped into him in the supermarket a few months after the funeral. And to me, others said, 'You need to move on', or 'You have two other children'.

A few months after Christopher's death, a stranger asked me how many children I had.

'Three, no, sorry, two. Three, yes, three. Shit. Okay, I had three, now I have two.'

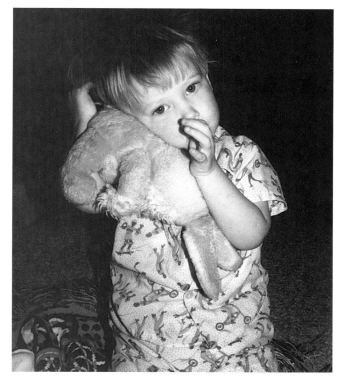

Christopher, aged two, with Bunny (1986)

My Three Sons (from L to R): Nic, one; Christopher, two and a half; Ben, four

Christopher with his football cake at his seventh
birthday party at Newport Oval

On holiday with Phil's family at Mollymook in 1992 (from L to R): Nic, six;
Christopher, eight; Ben, nine

First day at high school for Christopher (from L to R): Nic, eleven; Christopher, thirteen; Ben, fourteen

Christopher (L) aged fourteen, parasailing with best mate Ben 'Murgy' Murgatroyd on a Queensland holiday in 1998

Christopher, aged sixteen in 2000 (Photographer: Allen Koppe)

Christopher playing half-back for Shore's First Fifteen in 2002

Memorial Service for Chris Newling
22.10.84 – 30.8.02

I am the resurrection and the life, says the Lord;
he who believes in me, though he die, yet shall live,
and whoever lives and believes in me shall never die.
John 11:25-26

The Order of Service, with my favourite photograph of Cricket (Photographer: Allen Koppe)

Christopher's great mates Sam Chambers and Mitchell Coglan showing off their new tattoos

The author, Jayne Newling (Photographer: Allen Koppe)

More than 1500 people crammed into Shore's chapel and grounds at Christopher's memorial service on September 3rd, 2002. (Photograph courtesy of Shore School)

Christopher's memorial garden at home in Leura

Jayne and grandson Zach in 2013
(Photographer: Allen Koppe)

Professor Gordon Parker AO and Nic at the Black Dog Institute in 2013
(Photographer: Matthew Johnstone)

Happy? Can we move on? She wanted to know how I had lost a child and where in the hierarchy he was placed. 'I bet it was the middle child,' she said. 'It's always the middle child.'

I told her I didn't lose him. I told her I knew where he was; in a box in my garden. She walked away.

On the same day I went into Avalon to close Christopher's bank account. Ben came with me for support. The teller told us it could only be closed by Christopher. I said he couldn't close it because he was dead.

'I'm sorry,' she said. 'There's nothing I can do.'

I was shaking and angry. Ben demanded to see the manager and after several apologies, he ordered the teller to close the account. She put $7.45 into my hand and was forced to turn away under the heat of Ben's glare.

A friend's husband, a former policeman, berated me over the phone: 'Many parents lose their children. You've got to live with it. I have to face that suffering every day of my life. How would you like to have to pull dead toddlers out of mangled car wrecks?'

I couldn't trust anyone and the deeper I hid the more I became a stranger to myself. I learned to pocket my grief inside the dark cavity which used to house my soul.

~

By 2005 when we sold and moved out of Avalon, boxed up our past and Christopher's treasures and ashes, I wouldn't recognise my face in the mirror.

After we sold, we rented a beach house in Clareville on the Pittwater side of the Northern Beaches peninsula. Nic's avowal was prescient: If he died, I would have to sell the house because I would see him in every room. He just had the wrong son.

From the front, the white weatherboard was fashioned to look like the bow of a boat and if you sat on the balcony under the giant Port Jackson fig, you could pretend you were adrift somewhere out on the Pacific Ocean. It was a small two-bedroom bug house, the air filled with flies, the bench tops with ants and in every dark nook, cockroaches played Russian roulette with my broomstick. In this rental, Christopher was gone. I could no longer hope he would be coming home. With each day I found it harder to pretend. Loneliness was battering me and the unrelenting fingers of grief were clawing at my skin, ripping open my shell. I was exposed like an injured animal with nowhere to hide.

Nic loved living at Clareville, waking up each morning to walk along the sand, striking up conversations with the locals and visitors. Ben was still living in a small flat in Cammeray on Sydney's lower North Shore with Sarah to be closer to his work in the city.

It was a popular harbour beach for mothers and toddlers as the waves were small and the sand was free of syringes and butts. A step up from the beach were grassed areas for barbecues and picnics. The row of cottages along its length were mostly rentals or holiday houses.

I didn't like living there but during the first few months I made an effort to enjoy the benefits of the relaxed coastal living. It soon became claustrophobic and the noise of people having fun jarred my brain. There were people everywhere, day and night. During the day they milled outside our front gate, drinking coffee from thermos mugs as they searched for the perfect picnic spot in the shade of one of the large pine trees. And at night the car park next to our house was as loud as an amusement parlour. I jumped with every crash of a beer bottle in the council bin. I hated the way the waves roiled in like a greeting, then retreated like a disgruntled guest, rocking tranquil yachts, their stays clanging a cacophony against their aluminium masts. I hated the seagulls which begged for sandwich crusts and squawked when chased by little sandy feet.

I would never be able to listen to the ocean again. Before Christopher's death, it was beautiful, cool, the azure of a sapphire, a playground for families basking in the sun and tomorrow's promises. After death, it was a miasma of rotting fish and putrescent seaweed, grey and threatening like a warning. With a relentless nonchalance it crashed over my unconscious son, again and again and again, snaking its way into his mouth and eyes and nose. It made his brittle body rock and creak and crack. It made him cold. It suctioned his blood and diluted it to the grey of the sea, leaving him breathless, bloodless and lifeless. I would never be able to look at the sea again.

After Christopher's death everything became an ominous presentiment of the agony ahead. There would be no music but discordant bars which grated like a squawking cockatoo; no poetry, but inane iambic gibberish; and the colours—the blue-black of a raven, the rusty hues of a shedding cherry blossom or the coral of a budding rose—would be whitewashed as though viewed with boozy eyes. Nothing was beautiful anymore.

Nothing could make my heart yearn again. Nothing could make me walk out the door. Grief hung in the cage of my mind, a disinterested pendulum marking time with a metronomic thud. When you watch your child die, take their last breath, that moment will be marked forever. It will define who you were, what you are, what you will become. The past, every moment which came before, is a mindless, muted memory, an undesired gift in a camphor chest.

This is what grief looked like. This is how it smelt, how it tasted. This is what it did to me. I hid in a hole and was sprung like a shock absorber. I had no taste, no sense of smell; my view was blurred.

At Clareville the impact of shock dulled me but also made me vigilant to a doom I wore like a cloak. I tried. I watered the hydrangeas and walked along the beach but when I opened the front door all I could hear were the whispers of a gang of ghosts; all I could see were their silhouettes as they swayed in a heady dance around me. They mocked me, cajoled me and then with a disappointed groan, disappeared through the locked door, taking their melting smiles with them.

The hours were long and punctuated with panic. The outside was coming for me. I hid behind doors or closed the white plantation shutters but I could still hear the throb of life. I spent more time in my bedroom, at first in my chair then my bed, under the covers to escape the light and sound. In my room I didn't have to talk, listen or think. I could close my eyes and bring on night. When Phil and Nic came home I planted myself in the kitchen and pulled down my mask. I'd make dinner then plead exhaustion, falling asleep to their laughter. Phil could always make Nic laugh and vice versa.

～

It was two days before Christmas. I knew I was depressed. I was suffocating with it. I was splayed like prey in a spider's web, waiting to be eviscerated, begging someone to turn out the lights. I didn't care. I didn't want to buy a Christmas tree.

I used to love Christmas. We had a fabric Advent calendar with twenty-five pockets. A grey mouse in a red and white spotted dress was the daily marker and the boys would take turns to move her, Nic having worked out the order so he would always get Christmas Day.

Christmas used to be the highlight of our family year. Phil was home for several weeks and we'd plan everything down to Rudolph's midnight treat. The boys decorated the tree and placed presents for each other on the fake snow while singing and dancing to Bing Crosby or Dean Martin.

On Christmas eve and before they went to bed I'd sit them under the tree and light a candle for each while Phil took photos, their faces lit with excitement and anticipation. We'd hurry them off to bed with the threat that Santa wouldn't come unless they were fast asleep, but not before Ben poured a glass of milk for Santa, Christopher washed a carrot for Rudolph and Nic left a plate of gingerbread cookies in case anyone got hungry.

At Avalon in 2004, Nic asked for a Christmas tree. Daisy bought him one but no one could find the decorations and it sagged naked in the corner, and without any presents or carols it became the elephant in our lounge room and mostly ignored. All I could see was a six-year-old Ben in his button-down green pyjamas dotted with sailing boats smiling into the melting wax of a red candle and Nic, in blue, smiling over the rim of his. Between them, I saw an empty space and I heard my heart crack.

December 2001 was Christopher's last Christmas. He had eight months and four days to live. We spent it at home in Avalon and although we were all stressed and unhappy, we made the most of our annual family day. Phil lugged home an enormous live Christmas tree and, as always, we listened to carols and let the boys decorate the tree. Silver baubles dangled and fairylights blinked in a two-time beat. The cardboard decorations the boys made in primary school made their annual appearance and hung, a little bent and creased then, on drooping pine needles.

It was a very hot day and we decided to eat our Christmas meal on the back deck. We sat around our large wooden table, feasting on ham and turkey and something vegetarian for Nic. He was eight when he stopped eating meat after watching a bullfight on television with Phil.

The pesky kookaburra which I hand-fed every day dive-bombed into the middle of my plate and sat there while it devoured a slice of ham. Everyone laughed—everyone, except Christopher. I took photos that night. They showed Nic playing the clown as usual, Ben smiling quietly and Phil, open-mouthed, head thrown back laughing at something Nic said. Christopher was staring at nothing. His face was dark, flat, expressionless. His eyes were downcast. He looked like a ghost in the surreal aura of the camera flash. He looked scared.

I thought at the time that he was moody because he didn't want to be there with his family, preferring his friends or Ally and her family. I was hurt because I didn't think he liked us. When I look at the photos now, I see so much more. I see everything in that frozen face. His fear, loneliness and desperation. How did I miss it then? How could I not have seen his turmoil?

At Clareville, Nic asked again for a Christmas tree.

'Maybe next year,' I said.

He looked up from his hunched position in front of his computer and sighed. I knew he was disappointed in me.

I didn't think there would be a next year. Two days before Christmas and I knew I couldn't bear to live anymore. I was empty, lonely and heavy with guilt and sadness. The four walls of my bedroom were moving in on me. Phil and Nic were anxious. They'd gingerly knock on the door and cajole me to step into their world. I couldn't raise my head. I'd lost the will to even pretend.

A few days later, Phil begged me to see a counsellor. I refused. Then Nic tried.

'Drink this,' he said, holding a steaming mug under my nose. 'You've got to get out of bed.'

Opening the shutters he stabbed the window at the spot where the sun dangled between the two palm trees. He sat down by my elbow, denting my mattress with his inflated heft. With an insipid smile he touched my arm then bowed his head to mask his tears.

'Please get up,' he mumbled.

'I can't. Not today. I probably will tomorrow. I'm sick.'

'You're not sick. You're grieving.'

I gave him five perfunctory nods then closed my eyes again, hoping he'd leave me alone.

Grief. Such a big word. The very sound of it foments every ugly image I have ever seen of myself. I rolled over to hide under the greying, wrinkled sheets. He encircled my skinny wrist with his big boy hands and jerked it hard. He pulled at the sheet, forcing me into daylight. He swallowed hard, wiping his nose with his shirt cuff. His face cracked.

'Do you love him more than me?'

I gasped and shook my head.

'Why won't you get out of bed then? Why won't you live for us? Would you rather be with him? Is that it?'

'No. That's not it. I'm just tired.'

'I need you—more than him now. He's gone, Mum. He's in a better place. He's dead—I'm alive.'

I felt like I'd been punched in the stomach. He dropped his head into my hand and sobbed while I stroked the lank strands of his neglected hair.

'I wake up every day, Mum. Every day I hope it will get better. I never give up. What would you do if I told you I don't want to live anymore? Could you live with that?'

I sat up and hugged him tightly but he gently pushed me away.

'Is Criddy more important than me and Ben? Do you love him more?'

'I'm sorry, Nic,' is all I could say.

'There is hope, Mum. I promise you, it will get better but you've got to get help.'

I looked into his pleading eyes and something in me splintered.

He was right. He'd been through so much and was still fighting his demons every day. His brain was addled with strange voices, his vision blurred by inexplicable purple geometric dots which bobbed in a frenzied dance in front of his eyes and his body, blown up to twice his normal size by drugs, was ringbarked with lilac stretch marks. He had lost his beloved brother and survived his own suicide attempt. Now he feared losing me.

part two

chapter 24

There were eighteen concrete steps leading up to Ashleigh's room in Manly. She was the only one on a list of four psychotherapists who could see me during the Christmas period. I didn't want to go but Phil and Nic begged me and I had no energy to fight them. I also knew I was losing my mind.

Ashleigh's door was closed and I didn't know what to do. Should I knock, cough loudly? Unable to decide I walked up and down the small corridor to pass time then sat on one of the three conjoined chairs. I picked the middle chair then quickly changed my mind, choosing the one furthest away against the wall. The office at one end of the hall housed an IT company and at the other end a male and female toilet. Next to Ashleigh's room was another with its door closed. I recognised the name on the plaque as being the counsellor who saw many of Christopher's friends in the days after his death. I hoped she wouldn't come out. I didn't want to see her and even though she wouldn't have known who I was, I didn't want her to lay eyes on me. I was petrified. I didn't want to talk. I didn't want to go through it all again with Ashleigh or anyone else. Everything was stored inside of me and I was scared to unpack it. What would happen then? If I confessed, would I break down? Would I be committed? I had a fear of hospitals, especially psychiatric ones, after seeing my mother and then Nic surrounded for weeks by the depressed, the suicidal and the addicts.

I heard voices behind Ashleigh's door. It would open in a minute. I straightened myself and pulled up my mask. I had to be strong so I wouldn't cry. If I cried, shed even one tear, I knew I'd never stop.

Her door opened briskly as she whispered a goodbye to her last patient. She stared at me intently then beckoned me into her small consulting room, offering me a seat with her big hand. The room was different to what I had expected. There was no desk or leather couches, just a small square space, the size of a small bedroom. It felt cosy and safe except for the barred window, closed to hide the stench of last night's rotting garbage in the alleyway two floors below. Two stupid pigeons pecked at the glass, trying to escape their freedom.

Ashleigh was beautiful in an Amazonian way. She towered over me, her long, lustrous black hair framing a long, tanned face. Her dark eyes were soft but intent, intelligent but secretive. She exuded confidence and authority. Her long legs fanned out in front of her as she settled into her orange velour chair. She wore silver bangles and big rings and her neck was encircled by a silver chain, a black cross anchored in the tunnel of her large breasts. Her upper left arm was decorated with a small tattoo and her clothing was casual and bright. It put me at ease.

I sat on a pink velour couch which I assumed would normally be for couples. Dressed in black, I felt incongruous among all this pastel. There was a lime green bookcase behind Ashleigh's chair and on top, a moonstone fairy held an incense stick between praying hands. Next to it were scores of plastic soldiers and battered

Matchbox cars. In the corner on the floor a small sandbox housed pebbles and miniature rakes. There was a box of tissues on the table next to me, next to a stone Buddha and a white traveller's clock.

Christopher would have loved this room. Many of the spiritual items were similar to the ones on his bedside table. He would have loved Ashleigh, too.

She cleared her throat and looked at me intently.

'Start from the beginning,' she urged. 'Tell me what happened.'

To my horror I started to cry, great lumpy heaves that choked me. I looked down into my lap, wishing to be anywhere but here.

'My son committed suicide.'

Hearing the words out loud for the first time shocked me. I looked at her. Her eyes wrinkled with concern and she encouraged me to continue.

'He jumped off a cliff.'

'What was his name?'

'Cricket. Christopher. Everyone calls him Cricket … called him Cricket.'

'Do you know why?'

I started to tell her the origin of the moniker but she interrupted me with a raised hand.

'I meant why he killed himself.'

I shook my head and cried more tears.

For the next hour I told her everything, his depression and anxiety, Nic's mental illness and all that happened on August 29th, 2002.

I checked the clock—midday—my time was up. I was exhausted and drained and I never wanted to come back. I stood to leave but she asked me to wait.

'We need to talk about how you feel,' she said.

Oh God, don't ask me that, I thought.

'Just for a minute, then you can go.'

I doubled over and started crying again. Would this ever stop? I knew this would happen. I knew this was the wrong thing to do. She cleared her throat, forcing me to face her.

'Please. Go on.'

'I feel guilty,' I finally managed, shocked by my confession. 'I failed my son. I should have been able to keep him alive. I was trying so hard to save Nic I didn't think about Cricket. I really didn't think he would ever do that. He was the charismatic, popular one; everyone wanted to be around him.'

My words were spilling out of me, tripping over each other. I couldn't get them out fast enough.

'Whatever Cricket did, everyone copied. Why would he want to die when he was so admired and loved? Do you see? Do you see what I mean? Do you understand why I blame myself?'

'I understand that's how you feel,' she said softly. 'But it's not your fault. You're not God. He made his choice, you didn't make it for him.'

I slumped in the chair, indicating I'd had enough. She opened her diary and thumbed through the pages. I picked up my handbag and thanked her.

'I can see you at the same time next week.'

I hesitated by the door and shook my head.

'Eleven next Thursday,' she said then wrote my name in the diary and smiled as I disappeared behind the door.

From Christopher's diary: January 18th, 2002

The toughest part of getting to the top of a ladder is getting through the crowd at the bottom.

ANON.

chapter 25

It's raining in the mountains today. A thick mist has rolled in, turning the garden outside my study window into a secret fairyland. Two days ago my niece Hannah celebrated her twenty-first birthday and my nephew Joel is on the doorstep of turning seventeen. I can't help but look at him and compare him to Christopher. Although different in looks—Joel is dark—I am still reminded of the size and shape and manner of a seventeen-year-old. Joel is handsome and has the same charisma of the cousin he does not remember. There is a photograph on their fridge of Christopher carrying a five-year-old Joel on his shoulders. That is his only memory besides Christopher's surfboard which Joel inherited.

When Nic turned seventeen, I had the mixed emotions of gratitude that he was still alive and despair that he was the same age Christopher would always be. I had hoped Nic would be cured of his illness by then and back at school, studying overtime to make up for the years he had missed so he could achieve his goal of becoming a veterinarian. But he was still plagued by highs and lows, his brain befuddled by mind-altering drugs. There were many moments when his wit and intelligence surfaced but usually he'd either be depressed, irritable and tired, or manic and ready to take on the world.

After six months at Clareville we moved to another rental in nearby Newport. It was a bigger house which, in several places on the wide upper and lower decks, overlooked the beach. Although it was two headlands away from where Christopher died, I avoided looking out to the east where the ocean was bookended by towering cliffs.

It was while living here that Nic found part-time work with a computer company. The rest of the time he slept and watched video podcasts about new computer products or comedy shows on TV.

On the day of Nic's eighteenth birthday he was still sleeping in his messy bedroom even though it was lunchtime. He would wake up soon and want breakfast. Clowny was eighteen, too. I snuck into his room and gently tugged Clowny from the crook of his heavy arm. Its hat needed to be repaired and it would be my birthday surprise for them both.

He eventually sauntered out and I hugged him and wished him a happy birthday.

What's for breakfast?

What do you want?

What do you want to make me?

I don't mind. Whatever you want.

Poached eggs?

Okay.

One or two?

Two would be good.

Eat it at the table.

I will.

Now, before it gets cold.

I will, I will.
You also need to clean up your room today.
Okay.
I mean it.
I told you I would.
You said that yesterday.
Yeah, yeah, yeah. I'm going out to get a coffee. Want one?
Your room!
Do you want one or not?
Okay.
Want to come with me?
No, thanks.
Why?
I don't want to run into anyone.
Got to face it sometime, Mum.
No, I don't.
You do. You can't hide forever.
I'm not hiding.
What are you doing then?
I just … I like being on my own.
You can't do that forever.
Yes I can.
What are you scared of?
It's the way they look at me.
Like?
Um. Pity. Sometimes they cross the road.
They probably don't know what to say.
How about—'How are you?'
You'd just say you're fine, like you always do.

No I don't.

Yes you do. You even say that to me and Ben and Dad.

What else am I supposed to say? What would you like me to say?

Just be honest.

Okay. I feel like shit. I don't want to leave the house and I don't want to talk to anyone. I don't want to get out of bed. I don't want to make you breakfast, lunch and dinner and I don't want to look at your messy room.

Keep the door closed then.

Or, you could make me happy and clean it.

That won't make you happy.

Yes it will.

Wanna watch a movie with me?

Which one?

You choose.

No, you choose. I don't mind. Not that one, though. I've seen it.

What about this one?

What's it about?

It's hysterical. It's my favourite. *Anchorman* with Ronnnnnnnnnn Burgundy.

Who's in it?

Will Ferrell.

I'm not in the mood for comedy.

You'll love it. Trust me.

What did you think?

It was funny, in parts.

I didn't hear you laughing.

I was, internally.

Laughing's good for you.

So they say.

No, really. It releases a chemical—endorphin—that lifts you.

So does whisky.

Yeah, maybe, but that doesn't last long.

Nothing does. Nothing is forever.

God is.

Oh please!

You should open your mind. You may be surprised.

I don't like surprises.

Life goes on, Mum.

I know.

You don't want it to, though, do you? Don't cry, Mum. It's okay.

It's not okay. How do you expect me to do this?

By knowing that Cricket is in heaven and he's happier now.

You don't know that.

Yes I do—we spoke about it a lot.

You and Cricket?

Yup.

Did you suspect anything?

No. I was too sick myself. Want me to make you a cup of tea?

No thanks.

～

This was a snapshot of our day, each and every one of them. I didn't realise it then but he intended to be needy—he wanted to keep me grounded to life when I just wanted to be left alone. I didn't have the strength to care for Nic or anyone else but I had to stay alive to keep Nic alive. Somehow I had to learn how to begin to deal with my grief.

I felt like a barefooted tight-rope walker, teetering from west to east on a rotting elastic band. East was my intense love for Nic; west, my anger, frustration and impatience and my feeling of being trapped by his illness and demands. He was on my heels in every room, watching me like a buzzard. The Newport rental felt like a prison, dank and claustrophobic. I was a captive to Nic's needs, quarry to an illness which controlled our lives. I hated his moods, hated the lows, but even more I hated the highs which punched above and below my sensitivities. I hated having to be calm and reasonable lest I pissed off his twitchy neurons. I could see them conspiring in the dark caverns of his cerebellum—'Let's get the mother'. I wanted to reach in and pull each and every one of them out from their little hideaway, scatter them on the cedar floorboards and jitterbug the night away.

But I was so tired and it was easier to sit with Nic, talk to him and listen. When my lungs screamed for air and my heart coughed out its last comfort, I'd feign pain and he'd allow me to lie down for a while.

Nic loved hats. Gordon once told me that I was lucky because one of his bipolar patients loved Porsches and had bought four in one day. Nic had eighty-three hats. They were stacked in neat rows in his cupboard, faceless, headless but animate all the same. They gave me the creeps. There were two fedoras, eighteen beanies and a golf hat. He had four Texan ten-gallon hats, or shit kickers, as he liked to call them, a Star Spangled Banner glittered beret, sixteen ski hats and fifteen baseball caps with their tags still attached. He had a Chinese bamboo hat, two top hats and a bearskin. Next to the Mexican sombrero were a gangster hat and a boater, three kepis, four fezzes and a black woollen balaclava.

I didn't want him to have all these hats. They represented his mania and I would gladly burn the lot of them. Without Nic knowing I threw out the most garish of the collection but he found it in the bin and was distraught that I would do such a thing. I think he only has one hat now—a top hat, 'for formal occasions'.

I made Nic a chocolate cake for his eighteenth birthday. I was icing it when Nic yelled for Phil and me to come to his computer.

'I want you to see what Mitch wrote about Criddy.'

I didn't want to look but he pulled me out of the kitchen. He turned the screen to me and watched me as I slowly read what Mitch had written on his Facebook page.

'My best friend Cricket. You are the one I'll always look up to. I'll never forget you mate. You are my hero. RIP.'

There was a photo of Cricket and Mitch, arms around each other's shoulders, their snapped faces in mid-laughter. Underneath was another photo of Mitch and another friend named Sam, both wearing T-shirts, their left arms raised in a strong-man pose. 'NEWLS' was tattooed on their biceps.

I gasped audibly. I think my heart stopped. I tried hard not to cry in front of Nic.

'It's a good thing, Mum. They want to honour him forever.'

I nodded, told him I'd be back soon then ran up the stairs to my bedroom and closed the door behind me. Nic came in and hugged me as though I was a little child. Phil followed and took the other side, forming parentheses around my shaking body.

'She'll be okay,' Phil said to Nic. 'Just give her some time.'

'Want a cup of tea, Mum?'

Six friends were now marked with indelible ink to remember Christopher.

chapter 26

Rain trickled down the dusty panes of Ashleigh's window, leaving snail trail streaks. It reminded me of the face of a sad and weathered clown whose audience had suddenly grown up. Ashleigh sighed and I wondered if she was disappointed I came back.

'I'm glad you came back.'

'I nearly didn't.'

'I know.' She smiled warmly. 'How are you feeling?'

'Horrible. I'm really sorry, Ashleigh, but I don't think I can do this. It's too painful.'

She threw the tassels of her orange shawl tight around her neck and gazed at me with deep understanding. She asked me to describe my pain.

'I feel like I'm in a cage, like everyone is watching me.'

'Does your cage have a door?'

'No! I'm trapped. It's like a coffin. I can't breathe.'

I started to cry again, shocked by my inability to control my emotions in this room. It was as if Ashleigh was holding my heart in the palm of one hand and with the other, unpicking its seams with a darning needle. I didn't cry at the funeral, the memorial service or even on the night Christopher died. Why now? Why after all this time? Who gave her the key to my soul? She handed me a box of tissues.

'I don't want to do this anymore, Ashleigh. I don't want to grieve. It's much easier to keep it inside.'

She waited then took a sip of her coffee. She looked at me again but said nothing.

Time went by so slowly in this little room. There were too many empty moments, seconds, sometimes minutes while Ashleigh waited for me to continue. The silences were excruciating. All I could hear was her slow, steady breath and the clock ticking every second beside me. I'd look at it constantly, willing it to go faster. I knew she didn't want to interrupt my thoughts but I was loath to express them. She smiled again, a big, open warmth of kindness. She was about thirty, much younger than me, taller and bigger, strong and maternal. I wanted her to wrap me in a blanket, cradle me in her lap while stroking my hair. She possessed everything I may once have had and lost: confidence, warmth and empathy.

'I'm tired,' I eventually said.

She nodded and urged me to continue.

'I don't want to live this life. I'm too tired to be a wife, a friend, a daughter, a sister. I'm tired of pretending.'

'In what way?'

'Pretending I'm okay. Pretending that I want to be a mother again, that I'm capable of being a mother, taking care of Nic. Pretending that I still enjoy making pikelets with homemade raspberry jam.'

'What are you afraid of?'

'That I'll burn them.'

'Which illustrates what? That you'll fail?'

'Yes. Again. I don't want to be responsible. I don't want to be judged. I don't want to be watched. I don't want to take the risk of falling over again. I'm tired of accommodating everyone's hopes for me.'

A fresh round of sobbing spewed out of me. It was ten minutes before midday and I begged to be given an early mark. She smiled sadly and made an appointment for 11:00 a.m. the following week.

From Christopher's diary: January 20th, 2002

Be this the whetstone of your sword: let grief
Convert to anger; blunt not the heart, enrage it.

WILLIAM SHAKESPEARE, *MACBETH*

chapter 27

~

I woke with a scream on a cold night in our Newport rental. I'd been running in the woods looking for Christopher. He was a little boy dressed in blue shorts and a striped T-shirt. I was yelling his name. I came out of the dank forest and stood before a large dam. A voice boomed out from above: 'Go back into the woods. You have to find him.'

It was cold and dark. I saw a tall shadow moving in and out of the tall trees. It was my brother Jim. He smiled at me.

My breathing was harsh and my pillow soaked through. Phil rubbed my shoulder, sighed then resumed his deep snoring. I was still shaking, the nightmare slow to bleach through my subconscious. I stared into the dark, willing blue butterflies to fill our bedroom. Something didn't feel right. I smelt fear and I could hear the dread of my heart. I knew this feeling—heightened panic, senses reeling, skin crawling, guts contracting. The house creaked on its stilts. My heart bashed against its cage. I nudged Phil. His body jerked, then rolled over. In the silence of my terror I knew what this was. A second, a moment when life stopped and death wiped its boots on the welcome mat. Something was very wrong—something had happened to Nic.

The wooden stairs were cold under my naked feet and although I wanted to run, I tiptoed slowly, counting each rung, pleading before each new step for God not to take another son. The voice in my head was cackling. I stopped at the bottom, stretched my neck around the corner, cocked my good ear to Nic's open door. Nothing.

It was one o'clock in the morning. I didn't hear Nic come home from church. I crept down the dark corridor. Lisa meowed. She was on his bed—that was a good sign. Nic always took her to bed with him. I didn't turn on the light; it would wake him. He had to be there; he was always there, my reliable son. I patted my hands to where his feet should be. It was flat. I slid my hand up along his wrinkled doona. Nothing. Silence except for Lisa's purring.

Maybe he was asleep on the couch. Maybe he was on the deck. I ran through the house, turning on every light. He was nowhere. I ran to the carport. His car was gone. Back in his bedroom I turned on the light. His mobile phone, always glued to the palm of his hand, was on the bedside table.

I screamed, loud enough to wake Phil who came hurtling down the stairs.

'Nic's missing. He's dead, too.'

Phil hugged me, tried to console me, but as I pulled away I saw the fear in his white eyes.

Doom has a colour, a smell, a pervasive aura which encircles you and squeezes the breath out of you in dying degrees. It brings you to your knees. It is the steel grey fear of failure that binds you to your predicament but it is instinct which pulls you to your feet. Instinct, the maternal antenna which vibrates on a low hum, screeching when trouble looms.

missing christopher

Every mother's child goes missing—sometime. Every parent feels the thud of dread as the hours stretch beyond reason. In my mind's eye I saw Christopher's lifeless body under a tree, beaten to death on the Halloween night he went missing. Ben went missing on the day he got his driver's licence. A quick trip to the local mall to pick up his sailing suit took five hours. In my head I saw his car wrapped around a power pole, his body slumped and lifeless on the passenger floor.

Now, I saw Nic's body, washed up and bloated, seagulls pecking at his face.

When Christopher died, instinct told me he would live.

I called the police. I cleared my throat and swallowed the lump of hysteria.

'My son is missing.'

'How long has he been gone?' the policeman asked with a distracted, impatient sigh.

'About four hours.'

Silence. The background was muffled. He had put his hand over the mouthpiece. I knew he was laughing.

'How old is your son?'

'Eighteen.'

Silence again. I felt stupid but he didn't know Nic. He didn't know he had bipolar and had been suicidal. He didn't know his brother killed himself.

'I wouldn't worry at this point,' he said. 'If he hasn't come home after twenty-four hours, give us another call.'

'But he's bipolar. He's never gone missing. Ever.'

'Twenty-four hours, ma'am.'

I slammed down the phone. Phil dressed and grabbed our car keys. We agreed on our destinations. He turned left out of the driveway and headed south. I went north, past the memories, good and bad, of the small beachside suburb which took our child away.

The winding road along the shoreline was deserted at this early hour of the morning. The glassed facades of the exclusive beachside houses shimmered in the moonlight, mirroring the ebb and flow of the turbulent surf below. As I careened around each bend, memories flooded back of the life we used to have and as I entered Avalon, I braced myself, knowing I'd see Christopher on every street corner.

I drove slowly along the main road, squinting left then right—looking for Nic's car. To the left was the oval where Christopher had his ninth birthday party, played hundreds of matches and where he broke his nose. The skateboard ramp was on the right. Christopher's friend Troy lived three streets away.

I rolled down my window, calling out to Nic. Each street was as deserted as the last. I drove up the cul-de-sac where we used to live. A dog barked in the distance and a bat swooped down to the lone streetlight where it feasted on a meal of frenzied moths. Christopher used to walk Shadow up and down this street each night.

I wiped my eyes and continued through the remaining roads. I stopped off at the park and shone my headlights through to the play equipment. The swings rocked gently in the night breeze and several possums were having a party on the food scraps left under the seesaw. The large branch of the ghost gum, which played host to a tyre on a rope, creaked loudly.

I parked outside the birthday cake shop and peered into the window. Cakes were lined on the top shelf ready for pickup the next day. Tom would have a chocolate one, Andrew would have vanilla and Tiffany, pink icing with a ballerina on top. The window clouded with my breath. I wiped it with my shirt sleeve, noticing the clock on the wall said 4.00 a.m.

I'd been looking for Nic for three hours. I shuffled back to the car—there was nowhere else to look. I was so tired. Up ahead, across the road, I could just see the top of Christopher's floodlight. It was shining down to the beach below, making daylight of the rugged cliff face. No parent would ever again lose their child on that cliff because it was too dark to see.

I whispered to the light, to Christopher, to help me find Nic.

'What am I missing, Crick? Where should I be looking? Is it too late? If it's not, please help him to find his way home.'

I clasped my hands together and rested my forehead on the steeple. I couldn't do this again. It would kill me. I looked up to the black sky, the twinkling stars and to the biggest, brightest, yellowest one and begged God to end this nightmare.

The front door was open as I pulled into the driveway. Phil was home, waiting for me. He was hunched in the chair, his face in his hands. I put my arms around him and he stiffened.

'Drink?'

He nodded in that way which suggested he'd been crying but didn't want to admit it. I poured two whiskies and sat down next to him.

An hour later the black ocean sparkled with arrows of pink as the sun yawned above the horizon. We sat on the deck with a pot of tea, eyes glued to the driveway below. It was going to be a beautiful, clear day. Restless, we took turns to wander through the empty rooms, an ear out for Nic's clapped-out Volvo. A hungry Lisa meowed. I fed her without love and she glared at me hostilely.

We heard an engine and ran to the front door. The sight of Nic's car knocked my legs out from under me. I couldn't breathe. I got up and rested against the wall. Nic shuffled in and yawned.

'Where have you been?'

'Why? What's the big deal?'

'We were worried,' Phil yelled. 'You were supposed to be home after church.'

'I didn't feel like coming home,' he said offering less resistance.

'Why didn't you call us?' Phil said.

'I left my mobile at home.'

'Haven't you heard of a pay phone?'

'I thought you and Mum would be asleep.'

'We were!'

I was so angry I wanted to pummel the pulp out of him. He should have known how scared we would have been. He eyed us impatiently, accusing us with an indifferent flick of his latest hairstyle that we were helicopter parents—hovering and suffocating.

He turned to walk away.

'I thought you were dead,' I screamed at his back.

'Just because I was a few hours late?'

'We thought you were dead,' I sobbed.

'I'm eighteen. Do I really have to account for every hour? How long are you going to overprotect me?'

'As long as you live with us, we need to know where you are,' Phil roared.

'I'll move out then. I can't handle this pressure.'

'Do you have any idea what you put us through last night?' I whispered. 'You, of all people, should understand.'

'You don't have to worry about me anymore, Mum.'

'Nic! We drove for three hours last night looking for you. For your dad and me it felt like the night Cricket died. We thought you'd ...'

'I wouldn't.'

'You tried.'

'That was before.'

His face finally softened as awareness and guilt washed over him. Tears rolled down his nose as he pulled me, then Phil, into a tight hold.

'I'm sorry. I didn't realise. It won't happen again.'

'Where were you, Nic?'

'It doesn't matter now.'

'It does. Your dad and I looked everywhere.'

'I was at the headland.'

My heart stopped. Why didn't we think of that? Where were my instincts?

'Why there?'

'I was praying to Criddy.'

chapter 28

During the next few sessions Ashleigh forced me to unpack more and more of my grief and my feelings of despair. Although it was helpful therapy, I didn't want to come to this room each week to sob and splutter. I didn't want to talk about Christopher; it drained me and with each passing week I fell deeper and deeper into grief's well. I still had no hope; I still wanted to die more than I wanted to live. Christopher's death was my life's endgame, Nic's survival the breadcrumbs to the trap.

Ashleigh told me I was depressed. She wanted to book me into hospital. I thought she wanted to get rid of me.

'I can't start all over again with someone else. I don't even know if I can finish here and I can't leave Nic.'

'Then we'll keep going,' she said. 'But I want you to see your doctor as soon as possible; you need to be taking antidepressants.'

I reluctantly agreed. Then we spent the session talking about why I wanted to die.

I didn't want to live, didn't feel I deserved to live because my son was dead and I knew, somehow, I could have prevented it. I told Ashleigh I wished I had been kinder, softer. I wished I had talked to him more instead of screaming at him. I wished I had forced him to stay at home instead of letting him live with Ally. She nodded compassionately but I knew she didn't agree with me.

The tiny white traveller's clock read 11:30. Tick, tock.

'It's not your fault,' she said with vehemence.

'But you weren't there. You didn't see what I did to him.'

'What did you do?'

'I yelled and screamed at him, all the time.'

'Because he was a teenager, doing things he shouldn't be?'

'You don't understand.'

'Make me.'

'I said things to him—bad things.'

'Such as?'

'I made him feel guilty for causing me more stress. Nic was so sick. I told him he wasn't being fair to Nic or me. I brought up my childhood, my mother's alcoholism, my brother's death. I told him I didn't deserve all this and he shouldn't be adding to it.'

Ashleigh's face crumpled. Would she now understand? Would she accept that I couldn't live with this guilt? I was his mother and I put Nic and myself first. I was meant to love, nurture and protect him. I didn't push Christopher off the cliff but I might as well have led him by the hand. Women have died fighting for their children's lives. Where was I? Knocking back a bottle of wine? Where was I when he was so sad he was starting to formulate the idea of his own death? Why didn't the warning bells ring? There should have been a deafening peal when his friend jumped off a bridge several months before Christopher's death. I begged him not to go to the funeral but he did anyway.

That friend's parents came to our house a few days after Christopher died. We (the mothers) looked at each other for a moment.

It was as though she was acknowledging I was now a member of her exclusive group, one which no one would ever ask to join. She hugged me briefly and with a deep sigh, let me go. She knew we'd never see each other again. The pain had bleached her eyes opaque, her body was cold and taut, her hands as dry as her future. I knew she recognised the same madness in me.

chapter 29

A year after Christopher's death I bought a tiny miner's cottage in Blackheath in the Blue Mountains. Every week I escaped on my own for a few days while Phil looked after Nic. He was improving slowly and we both benefited from time apart.

The garden in spring was filled with tulips, daffodils, jonquils, snowflakes and bluebells. A large weeping cotoneaster spread its branches out over a dry rock wall which was home to Bert, the blue-tongue lizard. Tiny brown finches with red beaks darted in and out of the thick foliage while gang-gang cockatoos feasted on the red berries. Next to it, a giant chestnut tree was dinner for hundreds of yellow-crested cockatoos, the hollowed husks like hail on my neighbour's tin roof.

I found solace in my garden, feeding the rosellas and king parrots, and with nature on the hundreds of bushwalks in the mountains. One of my favourites was on the southern side of Blackheath across from the railway line where a tall waterfall cascades over the roof of an ancient cave. Another leads to one of the many escarpments overlooking the majestic Megalong Valley.

It was from here a young woman recently jumped to her death. No one knew why. A sad bunch of decaying daisies, strangled with a dirty yellow ribbon, was tied to a nearby eucalyptus tree. Whenever I walked to that spot I took a bunch of flowers and laid them on the rock where she last stood.

I wondered how she felt as she tumbled into the abyss, maybe hitting cliff ledges before her body splintered on the forest floor. This woman who once danced, made love and dreamed. Did she have any regrets as she hurtled through the frigid air? Did Christopher? Did they feel any pain? Was there a millisecond when they both opened their eyes in panic and wished for time to stop, wished for a revision of a hundred impulsive decisions? Or did they close their eyes and with outstretched arms, welcome the end? Not knowing Christopher's final thoughts would always haunt me. Often I will replay the last seconds of his life in slow motion but in the dungeon of my mind, the trap door is locked and just for a little while forgetting keeps me sane.

chapter 30

Ashleigh's room had suddenly darkened as the morning sun slipped behind a slow-moving cloud. It was a cue for a break and she sipped from the hole of her takeaway soy cappuccino, I from my double-shot flat white. I risked a peripheral peak at the clock which ticked loudly at my left ear. I had been taking the antidepressants for a month and I felt calmer but grief was still stuck in my chest like a razor blade.

It surprised me that after months of counselling I began to want to go to Ashleigh. Inside her room, with the door closed, locking out everyone else in the world, I felt safe and warm. I was still nervous and agitated but she could see my turmoil and taught me how to breathe from my abdomen to relieve my panic. Like a mother, she went through the exercise with me and that simple, kind and caring act made me sob, just like a little girl. It felt like she was syphoning some of my grief into herself through an invisible osmotic cord. I was so grateful I wanted to hug her.

I was beginning to feel close to her yet I couldn't get near her. I wanted her to cradle me, hold me against her so I could hear her heartbeat. I wanted to die in her arms. I couldn't stop crying and she patiently waited for me. I crumpled into myself. She tried to say something but stopped, knowing she couldn't be heard. She could only sit and silently watch my suffering. Professionalism doesn't always conceal a human's ache for another, and two tears dropped into her purple lap. If she would only come and sit next to me, put her arm around me—that's all. If only I could rest my head on her soft, broad shoulder, just until I stopped crying.

But she didn't move from her chair. I couldn't even hear her breathe and the clock kept ticking. It was only 11:30.

Ashleigh asked for a photograph of Christopher. I took out the one which I kept at the back of my diary. It was my favourite. He was sixteen and seemed so happy. He was sitting on a step, arms on knees, his warm, blue eyes the focal point. His right eyebrow was arched and his white perfect teeth were exposed in a gentle smile. His blond hair framed a tanned face. She gazed at it for a while then smiled sadly. I knew what she was thinking—what a waste.

'He is so handsome,' she said, unconcerned with correcting the tense.

I reached out to take it back but she wouldn't give it to me and I felt a flutter of panic.

'Talk to him,' she said, placing the photo on the chair opposite me. 'Tell him how you feel.'

I shook my head. She seemed disappointed and I suddenly felt ashamed and embarrassed.

'What do you believe in?' she asked.

'Nothing. You're born, you live, you die.'

She frowned then threw her dark curls in a flick behind her head and cleared her throat. The room vibrated with frisson, like a ghost down a long corridor.

Ashleigh asked me to go through the minutiae of the night Christopher died. When I had finished she appeared slightly shocked.

'What are you thinking?' I asked.

'I'm wondering what are your thoughts.'

'Time. All that time. That's what upsets me,' I told her. 'Why was he there for so long before he died? Why didn't someone take the time to ring us? Why was Ally's mother there and not me? Why at 10:30 was he highly agitated and by 11:20 had calmed? And why, if he was calm, did he kill himself?'

Ashleigh sighed.

'When someone wants to die and they've made up their mind to go through with it, often a calm, an inner peace fills them and the inner turmoil of indecision disappears.'

'Do you think Christopher committed suicide?'

Ashleigh nodded. I cried.

And the clock said 11:30. Tick, tock.

From Christopher's diary: January 21st, 2002

Every man dies, not every man lives.

WILLIAM ROSS WALLACE

chapter 31

The noonday sun hid behind the giant gum trees, affording little warmth to the white, saturated pebbles in Christopher's memorial garden in Blackheath. I felt the moisture seep slowly through my tracksuit top as I lay spread-eagled in front of his marble urn. The wet clumps of my hair were like deep cuts across my face. My session with Ashleigh had gutted me; I had to have a few days on my own.

It had rained heavily the night before, drenching the potted cumquat and lemon trees. From the back verandah I watched as the drain relinquished the last drops through a tiny, rusted hole.

I had planted a 'happy wanderer' over the wishing well I bought after Christopher died. It had arched over the top in a magnificent purple display. I was tip-pruning the dead flowerheads when something jumped onto me. I flicked at it quickly and the insect leapt, landing on one of the long, slender leaves. I thought it was a spider but when I looked closer, a baby cricket, no bigger than a five-cent piece, stared back at me. Its eyes were large and its little brown body tried to camouflage itself in the dry, crisp brown edges of the dying leaf. It chirped. It was a male.

Only male crickets chirp. They rub their wings together to produce the sound, repelling other male crickets and attracting nearby females. Crickets are part of folklore and mythology in many cultures. In Brazil, they signal impending rain; and in Barbados, if found inside the house, they signify that wealth is nigh. In Asia they are considered good luck and are sometimes kept in cages as house pets. But in other cultures, a cricket is a sign of death and is killed at first sight.

I have always been terrified of insects. I'm sure this fear was precipitated by my big brother's zeal to hear me squeal as I slid into bed or opened a drawer to find a bug or spider. It was an irrational dread I couldn't control and I spent many a night hidden under my sheets as a kamikaze moth beat its brains out under my lampshade.

When the boys were young I was determined not to pass on my phobia. We were playing in the backyard when a six-year-old Ben spotted a grasshopper on a tree branch. I gathered the boys around it and, at a slight distance, explained its body parts, its relevance to the ecosystem and its beauty. It suddenly jumped onto Ben's shoulder and the boys screamed.

'Don't be afraid,' I said. 'He's so cute. Just pick him up and put him back on the branch.'

'You do it, Mum,' Ben begged.

'He won't hurt you. You try.'

He gingerly raised his hand to encase the insect when it jumped over to my arm. I screamed and flicked it off before running into the house.

Night falls suddenly and heavily in the mountains, and as the last pinprick of light disappeared behind the tallest peak, wily ghosts dragged desperate fingers down my window panes. On a starless, moonless, soundless night, I drew the curtains against the dark, the crickets, the memories and pain.

I pulled a long, black sweater over my tracksuit pants and covered my feet with ski socks. I poured a strong scotch. I lit my candles and lay down on the rug before the fire.

The 1880s miner's cottage in Blackheath, 'Lavender Cottage', had two small bedrooms, a combined lounge, dining and kitchen and a bathroom with its own coal fire. When I stayed here on my own I'd light it then fill the old iron bath and sprinkle it with lavender and lemon myrtle oil. I'd turn out the lights. I'd lie down, my body fully immersed, and listen to the crackle of the split ironbark. This was the only place I could relax my body and my mind.

The cottage was canary yellow when I bought it but I repainted it blue. I loved it the minute I first walked into it. It was the same vintage and had the same feel as the green miner's house, also called 'Lavender Cottage', we owned in Wentworth Falls when the boys were little. We had to sell it to buy in Avalon.

I escaped to Blackheath for a few days every week. I loved being on my own, especially in winter when it would occasionally snow. I'd light the fires and watch as day turned into night. The cottage creaked with a sigh as the warmth slowly rose to the high ceilings. The fire's bright, orange flames reminded me of begging fledglings as they shot out flickering shadows on the walls of the hearth. It was quiet except for the crackle and the intermittent adjustment of the old tin roof. When the red embers turned to a muted gold, I'd drag myself and Lisa the cat to bed knowing it would be a fitful, nightmarish slumber.

For the past few weeks I had wanted to believe Christopher was in the room with Ashleigh and me. The clock had stopped at

11:30 several times and as soon as I felt convinced there could be no other explanation, I'd chastise myself for entertaining such mumbo-jumbo.

Yet Ashleigh believed and so did Nic; and if it was real, didn't that mean he still existed, just not in my world? Shouldn't that give me some comfort and relief?

I fell into bed and as I willed myself to sleep, I tried hard to remember how Christopher parted his hair.

I woke with a start, covered in sweat. The room was cold and dark. I pulled the blankets back up around my chin and buried my face into the thin feather pillow. Lisa snuggled back into my neck and purred. Her regular vibrations soothed me, slowing my breath. I heard something. Someone was here—in my room. Lisa raised her head and jumped with a thud onto the wooden floor before scurrying under my bed. I pricked my ears—no sound. I rolled onto my side and scrunched my body into a ball. Someone was getting into my bed on the other side. The mattress depressed. There was a smell, a musky, male scent.

'Who are you?' I whispered.

No answer.

'What do you want?'

I was too frightened to roll over but I knew someone was there. Then, just as suddenly, the mattress sprung back to form. I rolled over to find the space empty. It must have been a bad dream but I was wide awake and Lisa had heard something, too. I put my hand on top of the quilt. It was warm.

All you who sleep tonight
Far from the ones you love
No hand to left or right
And emptiness above—

Know that you aren't alone.
The whole world shares your tears
Some for two nights or one,
And some for all their years.

VIKRAM SETH

chapter 32

I didn't know I would crave my mother's love, her touch and her compassion until I lost Christopher, but her son had died, too, and her arms were as barren as mine. She kept me at a safe distance, too frightened perhaps to walk with me on the journey with no end. I tried once but just at the moment I was willing to lay down at her feet, she pulled back and went inside to make us a cup of coffee. I pulled myself together and never asked again. I couldn't blame her. I was just as cold.

I needed the love only a mother could give. I wanted to be swathed in a baby's blanket and placed on a fluffy cloud. I wanted to float—never to touch ground. I wanted a lullaby, a hand to comb my hair. I needed a promise I'd never be alone. Yet I was, except in Ashleigh's room, where for an hour she would care for me with her words, warmth and compassion. I wanted her to be my mother. I didn't think she had children but I wasn't sure. The only window into her life's private world I was allowed to peer through was the room where her new kittens played. We had our love of cats in common and they often became the subject when we needed a break.

An icy wind blew through the alleyways, disturbing the hamburger wrappers and foam coffee cups dumped into corners the night before. Winter had hit and I hugged my coat to me as I walked up Ashleigh's stairs. She was wearing black and a tired smile as she ushered me into her room. With hot coffees and my usual unease we settled into our pastel chairs.

'Tell me about some of the happy memories you have of Cricket.'

I opened my mouth but nothing came out. *Think, think.* An image came to me of him being hit while playing rugby. I ran onto the field as he writhed in pain, covering his broken nose. Another image of his broken leg, then his smashed skull, blood and deflated organs.

'I can't think of any,' I whispered.

Ashleigh cocked her chin and narrowed her eyes. I really couldn't and I didn't understand why. So we spent the session talking about my parents, my siblings and Jim's death.

I looked at the clock. Time—so slow in this room.

She looked, too, then checked her mobile phone. It was 12:10. The clock had stopped at 11:30 and I thought it strange that the red second hand was still moving, still ticking as it travelled its circular path.

It stopped at 11:30 the next week.

'What time did Cricket die?' she asked.

'At 11:30.'

She looked at me, to the clock, back to me, as though it was significant. I shrugged nonchalantly.

It stopped the following week at the same time and I told Ashleigh she needed a new clock.

'It only stops when you're here,' she said.

Yeah, right, I thought.

It stopped at 11:30 the following three weeks, and although I didn't want to admit it, the innocuous little timepiece was beginning to obsess me. I couldn't concentrate on the therapy as I waited for 11:30 to come around. What did it mean? Was it real? Was Ashleigh somehow manipulating it to get me to believe in her spiritual world?

'What's going on?' I demanded of Ashleigh.

She smiled and then explained that spirits often used time or frequency waves such as television and radio to communicate. My sister Josie had told me the day before that she'd awoken with a start in the early hours to the sound of her television blaring. I didn't believe any of it.

When I first told Nic about the clock, he said it was Criddy. I said coincidence.

When the clock stopped the following week Ashleigh suggested Christopher was stuck in the spiritual no-man's land and was perhaps asking me to let him go.

There had to be another explanation, a scientific one. Was the clock faulty? Was Ashleigh tweaking it? How could she be? The black hands stop but the red hand maintains its circular schedule. And Ashleigh seemed as shocked as I was. This was the seventh week in a row. Could it be Christopher?

'Is it?' I whispered.

Ashleigh smiled and made an appointment for ten the following week.

'Why ten? I always come at eleven. I don't want ten.'

'I have another commitment at eleven.'

I knew it was a deliberate attempt to vanquish the elephant in the room and I was angry with her.

The following week the day was bleak. I didn't want to go to Ashleigh because it was the wrong time. I arrived at ten with two steaming takeaway coffees. I was miffed and childishly indignant.

The room felt frosty and I was unsure whether it was the winter chill or tension and my foul mood. The pigeons were pecking away at the raindrops falling in rivulets down the frosted windows.

I could hear the clock beyond my left ear but I didn't care about it today. This was a wasted, pointless session. The room was morbidly still and quiet. She asked questions and like a petulant child I answered with monosyllabic grunts. Suddenly there was a loud bang. We stared at each other for several seconds—Ashleigh's eyes widened in amazement, her open mouth formed a perfect circle. I followed her gaze behind my left shoulder. The tissue box was in its normal position and the tealight threw a luminous glow over the black Buddha. Next to it my glass of water was empty. The clock had fallen over on its face. I gasped. I was too shocked to pick it up but I could hear the muffled ticking. Ashleigh didn't move.

The room suddenly darkened and my heart picked up pace. What was happening? I looked at Ashleigh pleadingly.

She righted the clock which had stopped at exactly 10:30, except for the red hand. Ashleigh arched her eyebrows and I shrugged.

'He's stuck,' she stated. 'Many people believe spirits can't move on to the next realm until they are sure their loved ones are alright.'

'I'm not alright. I can't live without him. It's so cruel. I can't say goodbye to him again. You can't make me. No one can make me.'

Ashleigh rummaged in her wallet and pulled out a purple business card bearing the name Penny, a metaphysical integrator. I didn't know what that was but Ashleigh made an appointment for me for the following week.

Tick, tock, tick, tock. My head a metronome in my grandfather clock

Pick, peck, pick, peck. The pigeon taps at a decomposing speck

Yes, no, yes, no. Let me go.

Tick, tock, tick, tock, the traveller's clock

Suspended time, death time, mocking time

A thump, a drumstick in Satan's orchestral pit

Bang. An execution. Still breathing, still beating. Tick, tock, tick, tock

On its face—faceless—the winders, the twisters, the dials

Daggers in its back.

Ha, hee, hee ha. It's just a clock.

Inanimate, but obdurate like a toddler

Then, as time passes, as time should, an inebriated teenager, the table, the cold pavement outside a pub late on a Saturday night

Tick, tock, tick, tock, tick, tock.

chapter 33

~~~

Penny had a mass of strawberry blonde, crinkled hair which she tried to contain with a large leather clasp on the top of her head. Wisps escaped around her lined face, softening her jawline, making her appear younger than her professed sixty years. She was lean but curvaceous, her large breasts visible underneath a sheer, white blouse. An auburn skirt, which flowed to her sandalled feet, completed the archetypal image of a spiritual woman. She smiled warmly as I tentatively stepped into her anteroom. She then led me into her consulting room which was dusky and warm. A shard of silver light shot through the window which was sheathed in burgundy silk. Like a pregnant woman, it filled and puffed at the whim of the harbour breeze. A massage table, covered with crisp cotton sheets, faced the panorama. I wanted to crawl between the layers and sleep forever.

Penny sat me at a small, round table covered in a batik cloth. She sensed my nervousness and fear and patted me on the hand like a grandmother. She wanted to know why I was here.

'Ashleigh made me.'

She smiled with a wrinkled brow then held my hand. She stared deeply into my eyes and I began to cry.

'What happened to you?' she whispered gently.

'My son died.'

'How?'

'He killed himself.'

Her face puckered but she wasn't shocked. She had probably heard this many times before.

I headlined the chapters of my agony and the clock sessions with Ashleigh which had left me confused and vulnerable.

'He's in limbo,' she said with force.

'What do you mean?'

'He's stuck in earth's realm. He can't move onto the next realm without a body. His soul is floating aimlessly.'

'Why can't he go?' I sobbed, swiping my nose on the proffered tissue.

'Because he needs you to let him go.'

I felt tricked. She sounded like Ashleigh. Had the two conspired?

'I don't want to,' I mumbled to my chest.

Suddenly there was a loud rap in the corner of the ceiling. We both looked up.

'What was that?' I gasped, my heart thumping furiously.

'I don't know.' She looked genuinely perplexed.

It sounded again, louder, then again and again and again. It sounded like a wooden hammer on a metal door.

'What's above this room?' I asked.

'Nothing. Absolutely nothing.'

Penny shook her head from side to side then smiled with just a hint of sympathy. She raised me with a hand to my elbow and shuffled me to the massage table.

'Lie down, close your eyes and listen to my voice.'

Tears streamed down my face and I worried I'd ruin her pillowcase. My chest heaved, my heart cracked. She relaxed my mind with her soothing voice while her hands, without touching me, washed over my body. Little beads, pinpricks of energy, surged through her fingers into my body.

I'd never felt anything like it before. It was as though she had anaesthetised or drugged me. She hovered at the end of the table and I felt my feet getting hot. I sighed and gave in to it. I was weightless, felt lifeless as my body melted into the cool sheets, the only sound my sobs as I fought against what would come next.

'Say goodbye now,' she whispered.

I shook my head.

'Say goodbye.'

I groaned, whined and shook my head, tears flying across my face.

'Goodbye,' she chanted encouragingly. 'Goodbye, Christopher.'

I couldn't open my mouth.

'He's here with us now,' she said. 'I can see him. He's a six-year-old with bright blue eyes and blond hair.'

Oh God. No! My hands were shaking and I'd broken out into a sweat. A breeze escaped the confines of the silk curtains and swept up my still body, raising the hairs on my arms and legs. In a hushed whisper Penny described Christopher, his demeanour, his soft, gentle personality, his fears, beliefs and insecurities. How could she have known all that?

'He is here next to me. He is saying goodbye.'

No, Crick. Don't go. Don't go! I'm screaming in my head.

'Say goodbye now,' Penny said.

I couldn't move my arms or open my eyes and mouth. I was glued, trapped to the bed. My hair was soaked with tears. My head was shaking wildly from side to side.

'Say goodbye now.'

'Don't make me. Please don't make me.'

'Goodbye now. Say goodbye now.'

Goodbye, I whispered to myself. *Goodbye, Crick. I love you. I'm sorry darling. I'm sorry for everything. No, wait. Come back. I didn't mean it. I don't want you to go. Don't go, Crick.*

Penny cleared her throat and the moment vanished. The room felt empty and cold, like waking up in an operating theatre. Minutes passed in silence. I finally opened my swollen eyes. I was exhausted, dazed and empty.

Penny was waiting for me at her batik table. She gazed at me then helped me to stand. She led me to a chair. I was so drained I could hardly walk.

'Sit for a while,' she said. 'I'll make us a pot of herbal tea.'

When I eventually gathered the strength to leave, I felt like I'd been raped. I stumbled down the stairs into the glaring sunlight. Phil was waiting for me across the road and ran to me when I appeared on the front step. I had a strong headache and I knew by his look of concern that I was deathly pale.

On the way home I told him Penny made me say goodbye to our son. He smiled sadly as he grabbed hold of my hand.

'Don't cry anymore, buddy,' he said. 'You'll get a migraine.'

I laid my head back against the seat and closed my eyes. I couldn't stop crying. I felt like I'd just lost another child.

From Christopher's diary: February 10th, 2002

May the road rise to meet you, may the wind always be at your back. May the sun shine warm upon your face, the rain fall soft upon your fields. And until we meet again may God hold you in the palm of his hand.

IRISH BLESSING — ST PATRICK

chapter 34

~

Outside the poster shop next to Ashleigh's building, a shell of a man looked at the world from a hideous angle. He was slumped in an automatic wheelchair. On his lap, and tied with chicken wire to the arm rests, was a rustic donation box which doubled as a security bar. His legs had atrophied into broken twigs, his hands clawed, one in a victory sign, the other pointed permanently to heaven. His tongue hung out of his lolling head which banged at intervals against the rim of the dirty sheepskin-lined chair. He was placed in front of the window, perhaps all day, until someone came to wheel him home. Marilyn Monroe was pouting behind him and John Wayne had a gun to the disabled man's head.

I put a coin into the box and it jingled, reverberating against all sides of the empty cavity. He didn't notice and he didn't smile. I ran up the stairs to Ashleigh's room.

I told her about the session with Penny and how distressing it had been. Saying goodbye again to Christopher had been one of the hardest choices of my life. I knew I had to let him go but I did it for him, not for me. It was a decision I knew I'd regret forever.

But I was glad to be back in her room and back with the clock.

'Is the man in the wheelchair always there?' I asked her.

'Mostly but not always in the same doorway.'

'That could have been Cricket.'

She cocked her head.

'One centimetre this way or that. He would have been a vegetable.'

'How do you feel about that?'

'I'm very grateful. He would have hated being in that state. He lived for his sport, being active.'

'He would have been alive, though.'

'That's not living.'

I watched the clock and Ashleigh pretended not to. As it made its way around to 11:30 we remained silent. 11:30. Tick, tock. I stopped breathing. Tick, tock, 11:31.

Ashleigh smiled kindly.

It was over. It would never stop again. Christopher was gone.

I left Ashleigh early. I drove home and fell, sobbing, into Nic's arms.

'It didn't stop, Nic.'

'It's a good thing, Mum. He's free now.'

The next week I was horrified to see the clock had disappeared.

'Where is it!' I demanded of Ashleigh.

'It was old. I needed a new one.'

'Where is it? Can I have it?'

She sighed, told me she thought about giving it to me but decided it wouldn't have been right for me.

I sat down and sobbed. It was definitely over now. Behind her, on her filing cabinet, was a new clock, black, defiant and challenging.

'So it was faulty?' I challenged.

'No. It was old, unreliable.'

'Because it stopped at 11:30 every day?'

'It never stopped during any of my other sessions. Only with you.'

'It did stop all those times, right? I'm not imagining it, am I?'

She nodded wearily. 'No, you're not. Do you now believe Christopher is out there somewhere?'

'I don't know. I don't know anything anymore. I'm so confused that I can't even think straight anymore.'

Ashleigh talked about energy and its power and gave me an insight into her spiritual beliefs. I wanted her world, her clear views. How easy would it be if I believed, like she, that life continued on and on, that death shouldn't be feared and our spiritual world was rich and inviting?

Twelve noon. I left wearing my armour of scepticism, albeit a little bruised and with a derisory snort at the new clock.

Ashleigh and I shared a few more sessions but with the elephant removed from the room, it felt hollow and lonely. We talked about everything but the clock. She asked me about Lisa and I asked about the kittens she'd recently rescued.

The following week I bought her two gifts which I gave to her at our last session. Once settled in her room, I handed them to her.

'What are these for?'

'To say thank you. This is my last session. I'm okay now.'

'Normally I decide that.'

'I know, I'm sorry, Ashleigh.'

She opened the first present, a necklace with a large, black stone, which I was told symbolised spiritual beliefs. The second one made her smile. It was a porcelain cat with a clock embedded in the centre. She thanked me and I could tell she was sad.

'I hope it doesn't stop,' I said.

We spent the hour talking strategy and coping mechanisms. At noon we stood together, she letting me know she would always be there if I needed her. I thanked her and walked out the door for the last time. I cried all the way home.

Ashleigh, the woman I had hoped would understand my strong desire not to live anymore, the only one I could talk to about my desperation, my deep, inconsolable grief. She, the one who taught me how to bear life, live life without the constant, daily desire to end it. Over the year we were together she showed me how to be a mother and a wife again and although I knew I had a long way to go, she gave me hope. I didn't hate myself anymore because Ashleigh taught me how to love again.

She saved my life.

When the hours of Day are numbered
And the voices of the Night
Wake the better soul, that slumbered,
To a holy, calm delight;
Ere the evening lamps are lighted,
And, like phantoms grim and tall,
Shadows from the fitful firelight
Dance upon the parlour wall;

Then the forms of the departed
Enter at the open door;
The beloved, the true hearted,
Come to visit me once more;

HENRY WADSWORTH LONGFELLOW, 'FOOTSTEPS OF ANGELS'

chapter 35

In 2006, our Newport rental home was put on the market. We had to pack up again and move permanently to our Blackheath cottage. Nic was twenty, working part-time and didn't want to move to the mountains. We found him a flat in the inner-city suburb of Newtown, and a flatmate, Charles, a close friend from school, moved in with him. We gave Charles our numbers and made him promise to call if Nic needed help.

We gave Nic and Ben most of our furniture, pots and dishes then hauled the remaining boxes to Blackheath. This would be our home and the first time Phil and I had lived alone together since the boys were born.

It was with a deep sigh that we settled into getting to know each other again. We still feared for Nic but we slowly learnt to let go and over the next year we were able to relax more and more, knowing he was happy and thriving. He got a full-time job with a computer company and travelled overseas.

I tried not to ring too often but I still needed to hear his voice regularly. From its cadence, I could tell his mind's state; he could never pretend with me. There were times he needed our reassurance and we'd drive down to talk to him or take him to dinner and he'd often come to stay with us. But he had something to prove. He needed to be free, needed to show us he could go it alone. He wanted to make up for all the childhood years he missed. As he improved, Gordon lowered the dose of all of his medications and he started to lose weight and regain his confidence.

He had been living in Newtown for six months when I called to ask if he was okay.

'I'm great. You never have to worry about me again. But I still need you, Mum. By the way how many tomatoes do I use in that soup recipe you gave me?'

'A kilo. Don't forget the tarragon.'

'You and Dad should go overseas. You've always wanted to go to Ireland. You can do that now, you know.'

Every time I heard his contented voice, the fist of anxiety unfurled just a little bit more. Phil and I learnt to breathe, to sit, to dare to dream. For the first time in years our marriage became the focal point, not mental illness. Over time, living in that little old cottage, making fires, going to dinner and playing music again, we discovered we still loved each other. We were damaged but Phil offered me hope and although I wasn't entirely convinced, I trusted him enough to grab hold of his coat tails.

Knowing this would be our home for many years, I built a more permanent garden for Christopher. Under the weeping branches of a pink rhododendron I made a circle with bush rocks and placed his urn on top of a mound of pebbles. Candles dotted the periphery and at night, the dew on the leaves shimmered and shook like darting fairies.

My bedroom, our bedroom, had a double bed, an old wardrobe which came with the house and two bedside tables. Under one of them I kept a CD player. When I used to sleep here alone, I'd turn it on before I got into bed. I only ever listened to one CD, *Natural States* by American composer and pianist David Lanz. I loved all the tracks but my favourite was 'Cristofori's Dream'. I only played it when I was alone.

One night I woke to hear the music playing. In the morning the player was switched off at the wall.

'Why did you play "Cristofori's Dream" last night?' I asked Phil.

'I didn't. I thought you had.'

chapter 36

~~

Time. What did it do to me? Real time, day time, the excruciating beat of countless seconds as a smile fades or the monotonous minutes of a queue of ants creeping around the picnic blanket on a boot-less trek to nowhere.

Time. Strange time, ghostly time, clock time. What did it do to me? Frozen under the carapace of grief, it made me look; I breathed. It took my breath away. When a day was done I'd package my pain in a picnic basket and haul it all the way home.

Home where the heart peeled and goosebumps heralded another torturous night. But the dark was a cave where secrets gambolled then flaked before the break of day. Pulled out from under the bed, I am sprawled, naked and withered under the beating sun, crows feet glinting, squinting.

Time has twisted and misshapen me. I don't remember who I was before time was just another day. I don't see myself in time's reflection and to others, I'm someone they used to know.

The surrealist painter Salvador Dali had an obsession with time, not real time, ghostly time. In dozens of his paintings, time melts, warps and distorts. Clocks are twisted out of shape as though squeezed at the waist by an invisible clutch, others drip from tables and over barren limbs in an arid desert.

Dali was Christopher's favourite artist. Above his bed hung Dali's *Soft Watch At Moment Of First Explosion*. It depicts the face of a stopwatch exploding. A fly is on the face and a moth, Dali's symbol for death, lies next to it. Time is recorded, frozen in oil at 11:30.

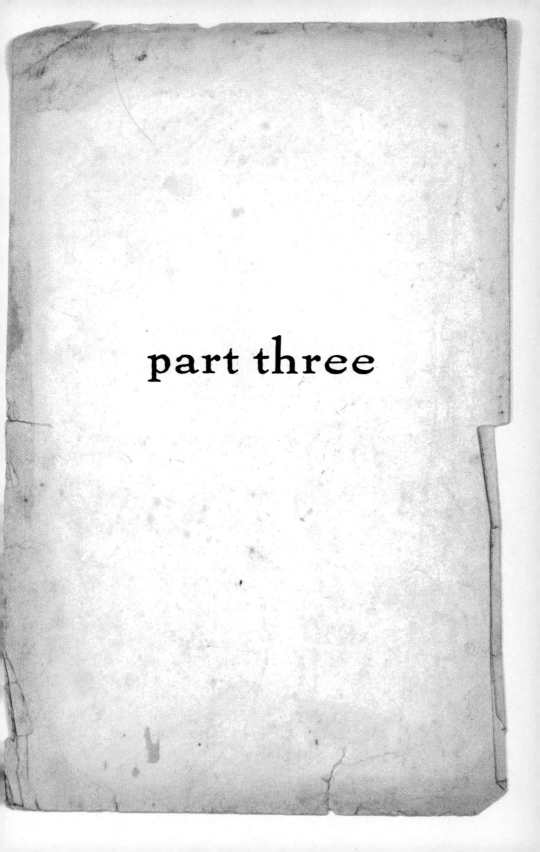

part three

chapter 37

A year after Christopher's death, I left the Northern Beaches and my family to rent a house in Leura for a few weeks. I packed a case of wine, my tracksuits and ugg boots. It was a small two-bedroom house overlooking a lush backyard, home to a well-fed ring-tailed possum and a pair of rosellas which I was instructed by the owner to feed each afternoon at four.

Phil, Ben and Nic were worried about me but I needed to get away, to think, to be selfish, to find some reason to want to return. I felt trapped by my grief and Nic's illness. My world had become a prison. I wanted to run from my life, to sever my relationships, to unshackle the ball and chain I lugged around with me. I wanted to be free of pity, of judgement, of guilt. Just for a while I wanted not to be the mother whose son committed suicide.

In Leura I locked the door and closed the curtains and sat in a chair watching old videos. I only ever went out to sit on the deck to feed the birds.

While I was in the Blue Mountains I decided this was where I wanted to be—here where no one knew me, where I could pretend that I was normal. Several months later I found Lavender Cottage in Blackheath.

When I look back to that time in early 2004, I am haunted by the frightened, nervous and suicidal person I was. It is almost ten years ago and as I write this, the familiar pain of deep grief and not wanting to live another day floods back, leaving me with a physical ache and a surge of panic.

I can also see now how living in Blackheath saved me, how bit by bit, day by day, tiny joys emboldened me to open the cell door, to take a chance, to breathe.

~

The white-pebbled pathway which wound like a snake to the steps to my front door was bordered by a thick hedge of English lavender. The pungent lilac flowers arced on both sides, the perfume lingering on suit pants and hippy skirts long after strangers had come and gone. I loved being alone there.

Often I'd stay under my feather quilt on cold mornings and I could hear footsteps just outside my bedroom window as pebbles were scuffed and resettled. I cringed at the insistent bang of the brass knocker. I didn't have many visitors. It was usually the Jehovah's Witnesses or my neighbour George. I would count to ten and wait for the thuds of retreat before I breathed again. Through the crack in the curtains I saw their disappointed backs and bent heads. Sometimes if I didn't answer the door to George, he'd come around the back. The seventy-five-year-old scruffy, white bearded, irreverent rogue was fighting prostate cancer and wanted to keep busy. I didn't want to get to know him and didn't encourage him.

He liked to fix things for me—the leg on my antique desk and a rusty door handle. When I was alone and a hairy spider snuck in from the cold, it was George who trapped it in a glass bottle. He asked me to help him fix our joint fence. I carried the posts, he nailed them back to shape.

I felt guilty when I didn't open the door for George but sometimes I couldn't talk, laugh or pretend and that was what he wanted from me. He knew I was sad but not why. He knew I wanted to be left alone but didn't think it right that I was. He was not afraid of dying and thought I was too young to feel the same.

Somehow he knew I was biding my time, praying for an accident or a disease so I could die and no one would think that's what I desired. He knew something terrible had happened to me.

George brought me gifts for the garden, a plant, a rusty wagon wheel or an old broken chimney pot he lovingly glued back into shape.

'Where do you want it?' he asked as he lugged it up the path, swatting at the pesky lavender. 'You've got to cut this shit back.'

'It smells nice, George.'

'Not if you're a bloke it doesn't. Anne will think I'm having an affair.'

He guffawed, which made me smile, and rewarded, he bade me farewell with a doff of his peaked cap and a pull at the old olive-green jumper Anne knitted for him many decades earlier.

At first it was a casual friendship and I knew if he found out about my life, he'd run away like so many of my friends and acquaintances who didn't know what to say or how to help. It took many months but he finally wove his way into my heart. I didn't understand it but I began to enjoy his quick visits. And, after a while, I noticed I didn't have to pretend with him anymore. He was a welcome diversion, and sometimes he'd come in for coffee and we would talk about politics or his love for his grandchildren.

'When my first grandchild was born, my daughter asked me what I wanted to be called—Grandpa or Pops? I said, Mr Macfarlane or George.'

He held his belly and laughed.

One day I walked him out and he stopped at the top of the balcony stairs.

'Who is Christopher?' He had seen the memorial garden.

'My son.'

He put his stubby hand with its dirt-encrusted nails onto my shoulder and bowed his head. When he looked at me again, his eyes were filled with tears. I told him what happened but asked that he keep it private.

'I moved up here because no one knows about Christopher. Here, I'm not pitied or stared at. I'm treated normally. It's important to me, George.'

'I won't tell a soul, except for Anne.'

The next day he was around with another gift and to invite me on a day trip with him and Anne, lunch included. I thanked him but declined. He kept asking and would use any excuse to check up on me.

One night I woke up to the sound of breaking glass. In the morning I noticed something missing on the wall. The iron candle-holder which housed five glass containers had only four. The fifth was shattered in pieces on the floorboards. How could that have happened? Each glass was lipped and held in place by a circular iron rim. The only way to remove the glasses was to lift them up and out of their holders.

George came in and saw the mess. He shook his head.

'That's not possible,' he said. 'Think you've got a ghost. Could be old Frank. He died in this room. Did you know he's buried under your maple? I bet it's him. He didn't like visitors.'

⁓

We became firm friends over the years, especially when Phil and I moved to Blackheath permanently. But by February 2008, George's cancer worsened. Unable to drive, he reluctantly allowed me to take him and Anne for his monthly tests at Nepean Hospital, about an hour away. I knew he must have been in terrible pain but he never complained to me. If I caught him grimacing, he'd pretend he had a splinter under his nail.

George loved oysters. Often, Phil would stop at the Sydney Fish Markets on his way up on Friday after work and pick up two dozen for George.

I knew George had deteriorated when he hadn't come over for a few days. Anne said he was very ill and the family, his children and grandchildren were all coming to stay and say goodbye. He was sitting in a chair and smiled broadly when I went to sit next to him.

'What's going on, George?'

'The bastard has finally got me.'

Then he bent his lips to my ear and whispered, 'Keep an eye on Anne.'

'I will. What do you need?'

'Oysters. A shit load.'

I took him two dozen the following day then left him and Anne with their family.

For several weeks their house was filled with relatives, nurses, carers, palliative volunteers and doctors. I yearned to see George but didn't want to intrude on this sacred time. So I just left meals and trays of oysters at the door. Oysters would be the last meal he ate.

Then on a cool day in March, I sat by his bed as he struggled to breathe. His eyes were slits, staring into the distance. I held his hand then told him about Christopher, the clock, the floodlight, the crickets.

'I'm not a hundred per cent sure, George, but if you want to bypass hell, there may be something more to this life than death. Just in case, I've asked Christopher to help you. For once, you can't answer back.'

I don't know if he heard me but he closed his eyes when I had finished and I felt the faintest flutter, like a butterfly's wing, as my hand left his. I kissed him on his rugged cheek and thanked him for being such a caring friend.

That night, George's daughter Vicky came to tell us he had died. Phil and I sat on the deck and watched as George was carried into the hearse. As it drove by, I waved to him and cried a million tears.

I missed him terribly. I didn't think I would ever let anyone into my heart again. Those beginning years passed in a blur where there was no hope, no dreams, just a panic and an interminable angst that I'd have to live every day waiting for life to end. It was George who dragged me out from the dark, made me laugh. George made me feel worthy and, without him, I felt a deep loneliness and sadness. I went back into my quiet, lonely world.

I didn't know it then, but it was because of George that the first seed of wanting to help the dying was planted. Five years later I would complete a palliative care course.

Then, a few months after George died, Isla came into my life and, in a way, I was forced to be a mother again. I had a hair appointment when Erin, the salon's owner, came in late with her distressed six-month-old daughter. Erin was distraught because she had clients waiting and Isla was too sick to be sent to day care. I didn't know Erin very well and did not expect her to accept my offer to take Isla home for the afternoon so she could work, but she reluctantly agreed. I put Isla in a papoose and walked her home. She was coughing and snotting and pulling at her infected ears. I gave her some medicine and a bottle of warm milk. She fell asleep in my arms. I gently turned her around and lay down on the couch; she was swaddled in a blanket, her feverish body flat out on my chest. When she woke two hours later, she smiled up at me, blinked her eyes, then nestled back into the crook of my arm. I fell in love with her that instant.

When Erin came to pick her up, I gave her back reluctantly. She thanked me and I offered to help whenever she needed it.

That night she rang to ask if I could have her the next day as she was still sick. And with that, two days a week became routine.

Phil, who was at first worried about me caring for a child, also fell in love with her. For two days our small lounge room was strewn with toys, blankets, nappies and a foldaway cot.

Soon she was able to sit up, then she crawled and finally walked during the period we looked after her. I taught her how to say 'birdie' as we pointed to the rosellas and finches from the large side window. She patted me, kissed me and was happiest cradled in my lap. There were times when she was reluctant to leave me, as I was for her to go. She'd bury her head in my shoulder to avoid Erin or Brian's outstretched arms. I knew this hurt Erin, especially, but

I was secretly glad that Isla loved me and that they knew she was safe with us and trusted Phil and me to care for her. After about a year, she was old enough not to pick up every germ and went back to day care full-time.

I had always called her Little Girl. When I went to visit her I'd yell out 'Little Girl' and open my arms out wide. She'd scream my name and run to me, throwing her now-hefty body at me and hugging me deeply. The first thing she'd say to us was, 'Can I have a sleepover?' She insisted on sleeping with me, banishing Phil to the spare room, and when I woke in the morning, a chubby little arm would be wrapped around my neck and two eyes staring lovingly into mine.

Isla surprised me. She wasn't meant to be a part of my life. I didn't want the responsibility or the risk of loving someone again. But she loved me and made me love her back. Like an earthworm she wriggled her way into my heart, my soul, and taught me how to care again. She didn't judge me or demand anything of me except love. She made me breathe again. With her smiles, her kisses, her unconditional love, she, like George, made me stop hating myself.

Then Phil and I went overseas, to England, Ireland and Scotland. I was nervous and agitated being so far from home and was sick for most of the five weeks we were away. We were in the beautiful fishing port of Dingle in County Kerry, Ireland, and I was struggling to keep my food down. I felt so sorry for Phil who, having visited Ireland with Nic a few years before, was excited about showing me the country of my dreams. If I didn't eat breakfast, I could manage day excursions. Phil wanted to try a famous seafood restaurant one night and I pretended I was able to go out. I ate a few bites slowly while Phil finished his meal. By the time we left, my stomach was cramping and Phil held on to me as we walked the two blocks to our bed-and-breakfast. It was a cool, dark night, the air filled with smells of fish and ocean. Street lamps lit the sidewalks on the unfamiliar street and, halfway home, one light suddenly went out. We both looked up. Without breaking stride, I talked to Christopher in my head.

If that's you, Cricket, make it turn back on after we pass.

It did. Phil and I both stopped and stared up at the glowing bulb. I knew then that Phil had asked the same question of his son. I squeezed Phil's hand; he smiled at me sadly then hugged me with a ferocity I hadn't felt in many years. We stood there and cried into each other's shoulders for the longest time.

chapter 38

We moved back to the Northern Beaches for a brief period in 2009. Phil missed the beach, his friends, especially Daisy, and the memories. We sold Blackheath to buy a house which had glimpses of the Pacific Ocean.

Christopher would have loved living there as it was a short walk to a track which led to the rugby oval and across the road to Newport Beach.

On the morning of August 29th, the seventh anniversary of Christopher's death, a strong southerly wind rattled the windows and whipped up the ocean into a frenzy. Rain fell gently, like snowflakes, and from the covered deck it looked like heaven was crying.

It was never sunny on this day. This day, every year, my head hurt, my heart was heavy and I had a deep clenching twist in my stomach.

Ben and Sarah, who were married in May, rang to tell me to look in the *Sydney Morning Herald* in the memorial section. I didn't want to. I waited. A cup of coffee, dishes, a pot of tea. Phil opened the paper. Looking straight at us, Christopher stared from my favourite photograph. Written underneath was: '22.10.1984 – 29.8.2002. You will never be forgotten and are always missed. Forever loved by the entire family. Your big brother, Ben.'

Brave Ben, oldest son, protector. I laid my head in my arms and wept.

Hours later Ben sauntered in with Sarah. He scanned my face to check my state then hugged me deeply. Nic followed behind, smiling while grabbing me in a bear hug. They hugged Phil then we settled down for a drink to Cricket.

There were fewer people at the headland now; some rugby mates, Annabel, Mandy and Daisy and Trish.

We stood, arms linked, and shouted out 'to Cricket' as we threw our red roses over the cliff. We sat on the grassy brink, all lost in our own thoughts and memories. The light went out. Even though it happened every year and we had come to expect it, we were still awe-struck at these inexplicable happenings.

Nic and I had been at lunch the week before and were returning to my car when he put a hand on my shoulder to stop me.

'Don't open the car door, Mum. There's a bug on it.'

He walked closer then turned to smile at me.

'It's a cricket.'

He gently picked it up and placed it on a nearby tree.

We were silent as we drove home from the headland that night. We were drained from the emotion this day always tugged out of us. Each year I prayed it would be different but it never got any easier.

At home my sons sat on the couch. They were so handsome, so different. Ben, the moral conservative banker who railed against injustice; Nic, the inner-city alternate, tattooed, pierced and a part-time comedian who talked to parents, teachers and school children about mental illness and suicide prevention.

I watched Ben and Nic whisper to each other and a deep feeling of pride suddenly stabbed me. But it was the pain of their missing middle brother which made me moan.

They both jumped up to hold me and I let them. I crumbled in their arms like an old woman. For the first time in years I felt safe and I gave in to them. We sat on the couch with Phil and cried together.

There was a feeling inside of me. Deeper than anger, louder than fear or grief, but I didn't know what it was. Then Ben and Nic told me they loved me. I told them I loved them, too, but it sounded different, strange, as though the words had come from someone else. I didn't recognise my voice; the words were full, soft and resonant.

Then something inside me cracked. It felt like my ribs were being pried apart, my heart, my lungs, hot and agitated. My breathing was shallow and laboured. I looked into my sons' watery blue eyes which were filled with warmth and kindness. I loved them so much it hurt. I always had but now I knew, for the first time since Christopher died, I loved them more than I hated myself.

chapter 39

In July 2012, Nic turned twenty-six. All he wanted for his birthday was for Phil and me to top up his savings so he could get another tattoo—this one on his right bicep. It took eight hours for the indelible ink to stain his skin and another two hours a week later for the touch-up. He came to visit us after his arm had healed and, with pride, lifted his shirt to reveal an exact image of his brother—Criddy.

On the tenth anniversary one month later, he showed it off to a room full of Christopher's mates who had gathered in a pub in Manly. They all agreed it was beautiful.

For Nic the tattoo is a way to keep the brother he sometimes has trouble remembering close to him forever. It is also a symbol of how much he loved and was proud of him.

Nic lost his childhood and many of his memories to bipolar. The illness also took away some of his future; he will never be a vet. In almost every way, he is now living those lost years. I still fear for him but not in the anxious way of the past. He has many eyes watching over him. Professor Parker, a psychologist, the staff in the local coffee shops, Ben and Sarah, his friends and Christopher's friends. Everyone is protective of Nic—everyone knows about Nic's illness. He has never tried to hide it and has never been ashamed of it. His honesty has been rewarded with love, understanding and a desire to help from all who care for him.

Nic is famous because he gets out of bed in the morning. He chose to live when he had so many reasons not to.

But he would never have made it if he hadn't trusted those around him, especially Gordon, who saved his life.

Teenagers want to be normal. They often hide behind a mask. It is hard to help them when you can't reach their soul. Nic laid his soul open and grabbed many outstretched hands. His dream now is to offer his hand, especially to troubled teenagers, those who have lost their childhoods. In his brother's honour, he wants to help prevent other meaningless deaths.

He still works for the Black Dog Institute on the positive psychology youth website, but some of his work sees him on the stage in school halls talking to Year 11 kids about mental illness and suicide prevention. In 2011, he was asked by a doctor from the University of New South Wales to make a video of his experiences for medical students. During the half-hour interview, he talks about his mania, his long journey to find the right medication, what doctors can do to help, the death of his brother and his long battle with his own suicidal tendencies.

'That was the worst symptom,' he states. 'I was constantly suicidal—every waking hour. I thought that was normal. The only thing which held me back was my family, not actively but just knowing how much they cared for me and how much it would destroy them if I did. I was at my lowest point mentally when Criddy committed suicide. It was such a huge shock and being at this nadir, my family feared this would push me over the edge. But strangely enough it was a turning point. Of course it was devastating and for a long time I was in shock but I was able to see for myself how it would affect my family if I committed suicide.

'In a way, being at Criddy's memorial service felt like I was attending my own funeral, seeing how the whole community was affected and how deeply my parents and Ben were grieving. I realised I could never do it. I had no choice. I had to get better.'

The video will be a compulsory part of second-year medical training and is: 'Dedicated to Nic's brother Chris "Criddy" Newling. 22/10/1984–29/9/2002.'

chapter 40

In one corner of my bedroom I have a box, an antique wooden chest with a lid that creaks when you lift it. Bunny sits on top along with Christopher's Buddha, his moonstones, a pebble he painted in primary school and a poem Daisy wrote for us on the first anniversary of his death. The chest is filled with all the things I couldn't bear to throw away. The cars Christopher played with when he was a toddler, his rugby uniform, favourite T-shirt, shorts and his red peaked cap. His first tooth, Mother's Day greetings and the box of meditational focus cards he bought to help get him through another day.

Each day he would put a card on his desk by his diary. On the day he died, the card read: 'Today I will focus on forgiveness. Forgiveness releases the past. It heals the pain so that you are free to dance and love again.'

On the day before his death, the card he chose focused on self-esteem: 'We are not alone here. We all walk the same earth, we breathe the same air and each of us is worthy of being loved.'

I also kept the Judy puppet he made in Year 6 for the Christmas Punch and Judy show, and the camera we bought him for his seventeenth birthday. He had talked about becoming a photographer after spending a week with his uncle Allen, a cinematographer, for the school's required work experience. And wrapped in a tamper-proof thick plastic bag is police exhibit number C87328A, Christopher's mobile phone and torch found at the base of the cliff.

Tucked in the bottom corner is a bag, loosely wrapped in paper—his ashes.

Only half fitted into the urn, the remainder given to me like a leftover container from last night's takeaway. What half do I have? The top half? His skull, his ribs, clavicle and radius? Or the bottom half, the femur, patella or his broken fibula? Maybe the front tooth that he shattered playing his trumpet, or the prosthetic marbles they used to fill his empty eye sockets?

I don't know what to do with his ashes. I could throw them over the cliff but then another part of him would disappear. I could put them in another urn and place it on the chest or on the mantle above the fireplace. I'm not sure, so I keep them in the flimsy package and sometimes I squeeze it, hold it up to my face and breathe in the charred, earthy smell.

When I picked up Jim's ashes, half was in an urn which was then buried under the tree in bushland, the other in a similar, loosely wrapped package, which I secretly kept it in my bedside drawer for fifteen years. I couldn't let go of him either. When I confessed to my parents a few years ago, I wasn't sure whether they were angry or relieved that they still had something of their son. I reluctantly gave his ashes back to them, keeping a small amount which I've encased in a silver locket. They buried Jim's remains in their garden with a plaque to commemorate his life.

There is another box in my antique chest with hundreds of letters and sympathy cards and poems from many of Christopher's friends; and another with Christopher's special items, love letters from girlfriends, a surfboard key ring, a fortune cookie proverb, important enough for him to keep: 'You have no problems in your home that you will not be able to solve.'

There is a notebook where he wrote down the meanings of words so he could remember them. There are only three entries: disconsolate—unable to be comforted in trouble; emulate—to try to equal or do better than; presage—a feeling of something about to happen.

The rest of the book is empty except for a quote on the last page, by American poet Ralph Waldo Emerson: 'What lies behind us and what lies before us are tiny matters compared to what lies within.'

There is a folder given to us by the school at the rugby dinner a few months after Christopher died. It was given to each player as a memento of their year playing for the First Fifteen. While each boy went up to receive his folder from the coach, Christopher's was brought to our table and handed to Phil.

The folder contains photographs of the team, the coaches and the First Fifteen Charter—2002. There is a photo of the line-up for the Newington College game played in Christopher's honour. Both teams are wearing black armbands and they stand, heads bent, for a minute's silence. There are weekly reports on their wins and losses, the last one written by one of the players. It ended with: 'Saturday, the 31st of August, will be long remembered in Shore's history as a day in which their First XV, against all odds, played their hearts out as a testament to a great friend who was always there for them and anyone he knew. As the last line of our team charter states: No what ifs, no limits, MATES ALWAYS. Thanks for the memories mate.'

In the rugby folder there are the articles which appeared in the newspapers headlined: 'Tragic loss overshadows Shore's courageous win' and 'Shore united in grief as players dig deep.' And there's a beautiful photo of Christopher on their last rugby tour. He is on a bus wearing his red peaked cap. He is smiling broadly, his eyes are alive; he never looked happier.

In the antique chest is Christopher's diary. It begins on October 15th, 2001. He lists his personal, sporting and academic goals. He strived for personal change, commitment and having a 'grown up attitude'. He wanted to be fit, give up drinking and smoking, and play rugby at the top level.

'Why am I off track?' he wrote. 'Frustrated, not achieving goals, no certain future, no track to follow, no mentors.'

On the page for October 22nd, his seventeenth birthday, he pasted a poem by American poet Nancye Sims which reads in part:

> *Winners take chances.*
> *Like everyone else, they fear failing, but refuse to let fear control them.*
> *Winners don't give up.*
> *When life gets rough, they hang in until the going gets better.*
> *Winners are flexible.*
> *They realise there is more than one way and are willing to try others.*
> *Winners know they are not perfect.*
> *They respect their weaknesses while making the most of their strengths.*
> *Winners fall, but they don't stay down.*

The entries for the rest of October described his up-and-down mood, not enjoying school and feeling down. In early November he had his second leg operation; the first was in February. 'I can't move much but I have a positive attitude to make legs good this time.'

November 9th he wrote: 'I feel sick. Had a blood test. Shit I've got glandular fever—major disappointment—worried about school and rugby.'

November 17th: 'Worried about how long a recovery the glandular fever will be. Still worried if legs will be ok.'

November 21st: 'Worried about the future. Did come to realise that all these setbacks (glandular fever, tonsillitis, legs) are all just tests for me to battle.'

November 22nd: 'Bit worried the operation didn't succeed. Feel that my physical problems need to be fixed first and if they don't, I will have nothing.'

November 26th: 'Starting to worry about shoulders also. They've been bad for a year.'

November 28th: 'Had fight with Mum. Pretty big. I got a bit worked up and said some mean shit. Bad day.'

December 5th: 'Have to have tonsils out on 17th. Want them out but I don't want to be out for a week or two from gym.'

December 14th: 'Felt down.'

December 29th: 'Shit mood. No motivation to do work. Bit anxious.'

January 1st: 'This is a new year. I will have quotes for every day of this year to keep me motivated. Quote: This year brings me delights beyond my most expansive dreams.'

January 20th: 'Down and depressed. Shit.'

February 5th: 'Down about my injuries—worried about weakness in my legs.'

February 8th: 'Saw school counsellor. Just talked. Pretty down.'

February 15th: 'Got in trouble at school. Had to miss passing practice. Coach pissed off. Went to L's [Leo's] for a while. Had some R [Ritalin]—felt like I should have had it all along.'

———

That was his last entry. That was when he gave up. No one knew. No one read his diary. I should have read his diary. Then I would have known.

Slipped into the pages on April 21st, the day his friend jumped from a bridge, was a memorial card with a photograph which read: 'We are all here to celebrate Matthew's time on this earth. A warm-hearted child right from his birth. He wasn't here long but we can all safely say, he blessed us all in his own special way.'

Four months later, someone else's son would have placed Christopher's memorial bookmark into their diary on August 29th, 2002. It also has a photograph and an inscription which reads: 'I am the resurrection and the life, says the Lord; he who believes in me, though he die, yet shall live, and whoever lives and believes in me shall never die. John 11:25-26.'

chapter 41

It wasn't just the sound of the waves, the familiar faces in the distance, or the memories of Christopher signposted, it seemed, on every corner we turned, that made us yearn to escape the Northern Beaches again. Perhaps it was a need to start over, an unspoken desire to turn tragedy's page. We agreed to move back to the mountains, to the quiet, beauty and serenity which anonymity promised. We knew we were running away again, trying to out-pace our pain but we didn't know how to do it any other way. If we kept moving, maybe grief and its ghosts would stay behind, set up a place at the hearth, and we could lock the door behind them. We found a home in Leura and set about starting over again. This time, we hoped it would be permanent.

I don't know the exact moment when the hand squeezing my heart let me breathe again. Little breaths, not deep sighs. Maybe it was the small things, a smile, a warm hand on my shoulder. Maybe it was a gradual easing of grief, for no one could survive that intensity. I knew I had to start letting it go. I had to be a mother to Ben and Nic. I had to let Christopher go and even though grief still sat like a sodden sponge in my lungs, I could now get out of bed and negotiate with dread.

My steps were slower and the days were longer but I got used to the habit of the hours. And although I filled them with feigned enthusiasm, I took comfort knowing another day had been lived.

The last eleven years have been swallowed up by Christopher's death. In some ways it felt like a hundred years but then no more than the briefest interlude of time.

I felt Phil and I were imprisoned in a capsule where a distant clock with a muffled beat heralded the passing of time. We could mark some big moments like Ben and Sarah's marriage, and Nic's improved mental health, but our grief was impenetrable to the outside world and we had found solace in the confines of our ersatz existence. Comfort came unexpectedly and fleetingly but we snatched the moment and dreamed for more. We still walked around each other and whispered with words we pretended to hear but every night, sitting in our candlelit lounge room, in the crook of Phil's arm, the thrum of his bruised heart was his gift to me. We made love but with just enough fervour to make it seem real without risking loving too deeply again. The anger and accusations were swept away by time's old broom and in their place came a contentment as dependable as our love once was. As fleeting as serenity may be, a wish to find it for each other was more powerful than the selfish acceptance of our tortured souls. We realised our union was the safest place to be. We were marooned by our loss but cocooned by our love and trust for each other. Only then did we dare to pull ourselves out of the past's quicksand into an unknown future together. Only then were we able to trust we wouldn't break each other's hearts.

Last night we sat on our rocking chairs under the patio heater watching the full moon peep over the giant pine tree.

'It's a gibbous moon,' Phil joked, knowing my fascination with moon shapes would result in a mild rebuke.

I groaned as he pulled me to him for a quick hug. The moon then burst into full view, spotlighting Christopher's garden with a silver halo. The gold lettering on his marble urn glimmered as a moth floated between it and the small spotlight which brings life to the grieving Buddha. We both stared at it then looked to each other with sad resignation.

'Are you okay?'

He nodded sadly then grabbed my hand.

'This is what nobody understands,' he said, clearing a lump from his throat. 'This is our life now. It stopped when Crick died. All we can do is make the most of each day and enjoy what we have left.'

And then he cried just a little and I held him.

'We still have each other,' he said. 'And our sons and grandson. Poor Ben. He's had to be so brave. He must have been so scared.'

I knew what he meant. Ben had lost his brother and had to stand in the wings, watching the tragedy of our family's future unfold. Would he lose Nic? Would he lose his mother?

Over the past few months and in short grabs Phil and I have started to talk about our grief. It is bearable now but we still fear our pain could puncture our frail hearts. I asked him if I could write about his grief. He nodded, seeming to be almost grateful that his painful journey and survival would also be heard.

'This is what it was like,' he says, handing me two typed passages, one written shortly after Christopher's death, the other six months later.

missing christopher

The heading Number One is underlined:

Crick was such a gentle soul who did not deserve to be frightened by his demons. He knew how to love. He knew how to care for others and, to his detriment, so often put others ahead of himself. He loved his brothers, his parents, his friends and extended family. He loved. He loved. He loved ... And then he broke my heart.

Number Two:

I need to talk about my feelings, fears, hopes and dreams. I have many photographs of Crick. I never know from one day to the next what effect a glance or a longing stare will have on me. Mostly I get comfort and warmth because the images show him smiling, with friends and lovers, or doing what he really loved—playing rugby. But sadly, there are moments when my guts flip over, when my eyes fill with tears and all I want to do is to hold him one more time.

He had beautiful hands—long and slender. When he was younger, he always wanted to hold hands. He did it even when he was twelve. I don't think he noticed that society and his peers may have considered him too old to hold his father's hand. I loved it.

I've cried often—mostly alone. I understand the difficulties people have watching men cry.

The first time I lost it was halfway through the morning after he left me. So many people were at the house, so many calls, so many flowers. I couldn't stand it so I walked up the back near the bush and lay my head and arms on a large rock and let go. It was such a relief. The second time was the day after. I had just woken up and my first thought was—oh God no! Don't let it be true.

I walked down the hall to his room, closed the door behind me, lay on his bed and smelled him. I couldn't smell hard enough, couldn't suck in what I needed. I hugged his pillow and kept breathing in. I cried out to Crick and then I let go. I was so close to him at that moment. I soaked his pillow ... then, peace.

The third time was just after Murgy showed me the tattoo of Cricket: 'Left side, closest to my heart, Phil.' Others had made the same incredibly sensitive gesture to honour their friend or relative and I didn't think another tattoo would affect me. Half an hour after Murgy left, I let go again. This time it wasn't a release. I had anger, so much anger. Crick had sold me out, left me. He didn't even say goodbye. I wanted to smash his room up, swear and scream, smash myself up. After a while the anger disappeared and I was close to him again. My life is definitely not a never ending tale of sadness and tears. I have happiness. I have love. They're just resting at the moment.

Reading this for the first time eleven years later, I burst into tears. I can't help but grieve again for Phil's deep pain and for the way our lives are ruptured by Christopher's sudden death. The ache and longing is never dormant but pounds when I look at Phil's pain, even now. During those early years we could see each other's grief but we couldn't touch it. We were scared of it for ourselves and for each other. We couldn't help or save each other.

We have the strength now to touch, with delicate strokes, the grief which has blanched our souls. Our love has saved us.

chapter 42

~~

My phone woke me at 5.00 a.m. on December 27th, 2011. In seven hours twenty people were arriving for lunch to celebrate my parents' sixtieth wedding anniversary. Nothing but the desserts had been prepared. We still had to set up the tables and chairs, make a beef hotpot, prepare salads and fruit and decorate the lounge room with balloons and photographs. But it all had to wait.

'Mum—are you awake? Sarah's in full labour. You'd better hurry.'

Phil and I showered and dressed in record time. It was at least an hour-and-a-half's drive. But Zachary couldn't wait. He was delivered at 5:42 a.m., weighing just over 3 kilograms.

When we arrived at 7.00 a.m., a healthy and contented baby was wrapped in the arms of a weary Sarah while Ben looked on, a little shell-shocked but with pride.

When Sarah first told me she was pregnant, I cried. I'm not sure whether it was for joy or my absolute fear that I didn't want to or couldn't be responsible for another child, especially if it was a boy. I already knew they wanted me to be an active part of his life. How could I love him? How could I open my heart again—take a risk that I'd love and lose another child? I was terrified.

When I first held him in my arms, I cried again. I'm not sure whether it was for joy or that I feared I could never love him in the way that would satisfy him or me. I gave him back to Sarah. And then he cried and my heart jumped.

I cradled him in the crook of my elbow and then, just before his body slumped into slumber, he opened his big, blue eyes and gazed up at me. Just for a second or two. My body warmed and my heart throbbed.

In that instant, that ethereal pinprick of time, I fell in love. I cried again.

During his early months I visited once a week, mainly to help in the house but also to get my fill of cuddles. He is now eighteen months old and our bond is euphoric. I still see him every week to give Sarah a break and for me to get my Zach fix. He runs to me when I walk in the door. His kiss is open-mouthed, his arms tight around my neck. We dance a waltz around the kitchen; he, the partner, in my arms. We sing 'A Frog Went Walking on a Summer's Day'—our special tune. I taught him how to answer 'rah' when asked what a lion says, although Ben and Sarah have each told me independently that it was for them he said it for the first time.

Our few precious hours together are filled with building blocks, Thomas the Tank Engine and wooden Brio train tracks, his obsession. I blow bubbles and he runs to pop them. I crawl from Ben and Sarah's bedroom to his room to hide behind the door or cot, shouting boo, as he first catches sight of me. With an uproarious laugh, he throws himself into my arms. We wrestle in the grass, tumbling over each other, the final fling a full-bodied flop onto my stomach. I grunt, he giggles. I pull funny faces, put his socks on my ears, saucepans on my head. Making him laugh fills me with life.

I make a tunnel with my legs and he never seems to tire of going through one way and then back again. He doesn't want to sleep but often constant play tires him, much as he tries to pretend it doesn't.

I wrap him in his sleeping bag and hold him against my chest as we read a book, swaying in a rocking chair to the gentle beat of a lullaby emanating from the tummy of Leroy the bear. He fights it and then looks up at me as his eyes flit and flutter and his body goes limp.

We play in the park, go to the zoo and on countless suburban train rides. When I have to leave, he often cries and my heart cracks, just a little. I miss him when I'm gone and I can't wait to see him again.

He is blond, blue-eyed and chubby, just like Christopher was. But he doesn't remind me of Christopher and perhaps that was my greatest fear. He is just as smart, sensitive and loving but he is Ben and Sarah's child, a mixture of Sarah's great beauty and Ben's good looks. He has Sarah's warmth and inquisitiveness and Ben's strength and stoicism. When he falls over and hurts himself, he wants to cry but an urgent cuddle and a kiss is all he really needs.

My deep love for him shocks me. I used to wonder why I dared to take the chance but now I know I had no choice. He weaved his way into my life, my soul. He chipped away at the ice encasing my heart with his unconditional love. He is my greatest pleasure. I'd give my life for him.

The wind is howling outside my study window, upsetting the currawongs in the sycamore tree and the male bowerbird who stole my blue tealight for his nest underneath the oyster plant. The screen door bangs against its flimsy hinge and the hanging chimes sound like an urgent fire drill. Doors thump, windows rattle and the shallow-rooted pittosporums threaten to topple in the strong southerly screaming in a westerly direction and over the high ridges of the Central Tablelands.

I have the fire lit and have buttressed the Edwardian doors leading out to the deck with draft blockers, one in the shape of a long sausage dog. On my antique desk an orange dragonfly stares at me with green eyes from the shade of my leadlight lamp. There is a photo of Christopher, the same one used on the memorial service sheet, and one of Nic, Zach and Sarah and Ben.

Ben still works in the banking industry and is getting ready to sail in the Moth World Titles in Hawaii. While he is away, Sarah and Zach will stay with us.

Ben is anxious we all have a Christmas together. He wants Zach to experience the joys of Santa Claus and the excitement of a tree with fairylights, baubles and gold and silver tinsel. And he wants Phil and me to be there, to be happy, to recover to build our new lives around his son.

This year, Phil and I are going away to New Zealand but I've made a promise we will have a 'real' Christmas next year and I know, then will be the right time. Then, I won't have that image of Ben and Nic sitting under the tree, each holding a candle, with a space between them where Christopher should be. Then, it will be just Zach and maybe a little brother or sister cradled next to him.

This is what my future looks like. I now know why I'm still here. To watch my beautiful sons forge their careers, have children, be happy, and to watch Zach grow.

After I spent another beautiful day with my grandson recently, Sarah and Zach walked me to the train station for my trip back to the Blue Mountains. Sarah had put Zach into his stroller and I kissed him goodbye as the train rolled in. Distracted by the noise and the opening of the train doors, he hadn't realised I'd hopped on board. As I waved goodbye he caught sight of me and, realising I was leaving, flung his arms out to me and screamed as if to beg me not to go. As the doors closed his scream became shrill and my heart broke. Everyone on the carriage was watching the drama and felt my despair as I wiped my eyes and took a seat.

I can't wait to see him again. I can't wait to feel his pudgy arms around my neck, his lips on mine, his aqua eyes, framed with long, blond eyelashes, fluttering against my cheek. Having Zach in my life will never fill the void of losing Christopher, but through his love I now have hope for the future and a desire to love again. His existence helps me to search for a deeper meaning to life and death. Watching Christopher die was shocking and frightening. No one should die alone and in fear. That, along with my experience with George, is why I did a volunteer course to become a palliative carer, and that's where I met Deane.

chapter 43

~~

2013

Outside the old church chapel, down a cobbled laneway, through a jasmine-scented arch, Deane sits hunched on a bench under a pine tree, waiting for something, expecting nothing. He rubs his knees then pulls at a dandelion, counting the petals as he tosses them to the wind. He closes his mud eyes and sighs the sough of a tortured soul.

He twists his yellow rubber wristband then scratches at the branded word HOPE, stabbing each letter with a jagged fingernail. He lets himself go, his back to the boards, his head to the heavens and his heart to winter's insipid western sun.

Deane knows death—death is his friend—death waits patiently, each day, for a falter in his footstep. Deane is only twenty-eight, the same age Christopher would have been. I watch his movements, a hand through hair, a raised eyebrow, the jiggle of his right knee, a sign of anxiety or despair I've cringed through many times with my three sons. He is a man but still the boy who put his head through a leather noose and with one long limb kicked at his father's stepladder; still the eighteen-year-old boy, who, two months later, was forced to remain naked after being yanked from a rafter in a locked psychiatric unit, his pyjama top around his neck.

His skin is still smooth and his dark hair still gleams but it is thinning and the boy unwittingly becomes a man.

Deane knows about death. His aunt killed herself a few months ago. It must be in the genes and he wonders if I want to die.

'I did,' I confess.

He nods—he knows how his mother's heart cracked after each of his failed attempts to die. He sees the way she stoops and shuffles and distrusts his proffered smile. He hears her anxious sobs and the fracture of ice as an amber river winds its way through the frozen cubes.

'Do you?' I ask.

'Want to die? Yes. Sometimes. Sometimes, often. It's there for me if I want it. I don't have much hope but I'm trying to find it.'

'Is that why you're here?'

Here is the church, the dining hall, the small chapel of the sisters of Our Lady of the Nativity where Deane and I have been learning to become palliative carers. The course is held over eight weeks every two years and volunteers are screened and interviewed before being selected.

'I know death,' he says. 'I think I can help'. He smiles at me, the lines smoothing a second before the turn of his head. He sees in me what I see in him and sometimes, when unmasked, we are frightened by what we see. 'Why are you here?'

'Because death is just as important as birth.'

'Really?'

'No one should die alone, in pain or in fear.'

'Like Christopher?'

'No. I meant the dying, the terminally ill.'

He smiles and looks away again.

'It's the same for you?'

He shrugs. 'I know death,' is all he says.

And he does, as do I. Death for us is hideous and ugly and violent like a rape. It slams into you, sprawls and flattens you like a paper doll.

'Why did you want to die?' I whisper.

'I was meant to,' he said. 'I'd been in bed, in the dark for two years. I didn't leave my room. Every day was getting worse, everything was unravelling. Ironically, the only thing which forced me out of the dark into the light was to die.'

He was cut down from the giant Japanese maple—saved—choking on the breath he didn't want to take. He went back into the dark, his room, his bed. Then he went mad. He was placed in a locked room with 'neon' lights, moaning 'cell' mates and nosey staff who parted his scalp to peer into his brain. He was dazed and doped but nothing could slake his fear.

'I couldn't think about anything in the outside world. I was in an altered state where my world, even though filled with pain and misery—was all that mattered. I was disconnected to life and the people around me, my family, friends. I didn't care about anyone. There were no consequences.'

'At that moment, when you decide, at that exact second—what is it like?' I asked. 'What are you thinking?'

'It was different—for me and your son.'

'Why?'

'Maybe it is the same in that we both wanted to die, to be rid of the pain forever. But for me it wasn't impulsive: I planned it—meticulously—twice. Everything was slow and calm. A peace came over me. I couldn't think of anything I wanted more than not to have to take another breath. I wanted to die and I believed I was meant to die.'

'Are you glad you didn't?'

Silence. He gazes out to the vast valley beyond a row of eucalyptus trees. The red fingers of the sun's dying rays splay like knife wounds on the rock face, in the cracks of secret caves and under the ledges where the homeless will light fires to keep warm tonight. He turns to me and smiles, a tepid expression of lost faith. He shrugs.

'It's different for everyone,' he says. 'The answer isn't always in the act. Sometimes there is no answer.'

'But are you glad you didn't die?'

'I still can't see the future but it doesn't scare me like it used to. The future is always worse than the present. I have no idea how I got here. I don't know how I'm still alive. But I am and for now it's okay. Everyone still watches me and my mother sometimes gets angry but there's nothing I can do about it.'

'Tell her she's lucky. She still has her son. Tell her she has a second chance.'

He smiles and, with the delicacy of a spider's creep, flits a consoling hand across mine.

I understand, just a little more, why teenagers decide the interminable future is too hard to bear. Their lives are lived for each day and when each day is wracked with angst, uncertainty and a heartbreaking pain and belief that nothing will get better, death can be their only way out, the key which opens their crypt and sets them free.

Deane saw no way out; he planned his death with spirit and, with an energising zeal he never felt with living, stumbled towards oblivion. For Christopher, life was deteriorating quickly. His body was failing him and his tenuous hold on his mental state was plummeting into a disquieting realm which housed his greatest fear. He didn't plan it like Deane, but the pain was as intense and as he climbed the cliff and neared the top, there was a moment, an impulsive second, where death was desirable. For Christopher, it was easier to let go than to hold on.

Deane and I walk back into the course's final session adjusting our faces. I thank him.

'Anytime,' he says as he throws his lanky frame into the seat next to mine.

While the others are settling he whispers to me: 'Dying is a release whether you're sick or in pain. It's a relief—sometimes, life's *raison d'être*.'

And then I realised why I was here. I wanted to have some control over death, smooth it, warm it, care for it. I wanted to blunt the barbed brutality of it. I wanted to lay death on satin sheets and stroke it while humming a lullaby. I wanted death to fade, not be pulled through a pane of shattering glass.

chapter 44

~

It has been raining for a week in the mountains and the last of the red autumn leaves have dropped from the giant limbs of the liquidambar. The bluebells, grape hyacinths, freesias and snowdrops are grateful for the extra drink and in a few weeks time, so too will the tulips, daffodils and crocus. I collect the crocus stamens—saffron—after flowering and dry them to use in next winter's tagines and curries. The birdbaths are full and it is cold enough in July for their surfaces to ice over into mini skate rinks. The grass is white with frost and the six chickens down the back of the yard aren't as keen as usual to leave their roosts.

The Great Western Highway is wet and slippery as I make my way to Peter's house in Wentworth Falls. My first palliative client, he is eighty and has brain cancer. He is strong, brave and funny. We have a great bond and much in common. We love grandfather clocks and antiques and both of us wish we had lived a hundred and fifty years ago when life was simple. He has a photo gallery of all his dead relatives on his hallway wall—so do I. We love to read—he on his Kindle, I with real books.

'You should try it,' he says as we sit by the fire in his small lounge room. 'So much easier. You can change the font and the size of the type.'

'Don't you miss the smell of paper?'

'Nah. Had a lifetime of that.'

Peter lives alone. His son lives interstate and his daughter in northern Sydney. His wife died twenty years ago. He is intelligent, interested, thoughtful and kind.

He doesn't like taking up too much of my time but is glad when, after the chores, I make a cup of tea and we sit across from each other in his leather chairs, talking politics, family and the past, his and mine. He reminds me of George and I have to work hard to keep a professional distance.

On the way home from Peter's house I pull up outside our old Wentworth Falls cottage. Built in 1885, the two-bedroom, one-bathroom green weatherboard has now been painted grey. The clematis I planted on the arched entranceway is in hibernation, its twigged fingers twirled and twisted through the wooden canopy. The paths are fringed with winter roses and daffodils and I can just see the old plum tree through the purple-spiked echium bush. Each year we all watched as the plums turned from green to pink to red and we were ready for the annual dash to pick them before the rosellas and king parrots took up residence in its arched branches. I made jam and stewed fruit and Christopher ate them straight from the fruit bowl, not minding the tart twinge on tongue.

The boys were young when we owned this house which we used as a weekender. They used to bring their friends and bunk down on mattresses in the enclosed balcony. They'd play monopoly or Uno on dark days but when it shone, we'd bushwalk to the valley below searching for the woody fruit of the mountain devil. I had a birdbath surrounded by miniature frogs and ten opium poppies. I waited all year for the double mauve petals to come into flower.

Christopher was thirteen when he and his mate decided to harvest opium. They beheaded all ten poppies, cut them open and scooped out the poppy seeds to dry in the sun. I scolded them but secretly giggled. It is the latex (the thick juice with seeps from the incision in the pod) which produces the opiate. Disappointed by the seeds of his labour, he left them alone the following year.

I often sit outside this house. It holds so many memories of our happy family in the time before the boys got sick. Sometimes a shaft of light will bounce against the red tulips in the stained glass window on the front door and it will make me cry. Christopher used to squash his face against the glass to make me laugh. Then it is gone and the memory fades and I drive home.

chapter 45

I know this much. I know that every day for the rest of my life I will be disfigured by Christopher's death. I know the memory of that night will always be a sharp fissure, a cut which refuses to heal. The picture in my mind of his alive body, tumbling through the dark air, will be the last one I have each and every night. His final thoughts will plague me until I have my own.

And as I write this, tears blind me and I know grief still lives, a fat lump of it just under the surface, a fine film under the mask.

After eleven years, I can't remember the sound of his voice or the way he walked. I can't remember his touch or the way he sat in a chair. I can smell him but only because Nic has taken to wearing the same Giorgio Armani cologne. I keep the almost empty bottle, which I found in Christopher's rugby bag, in the drawer next to my bed. When I need to, I inhale it deeply and for a moment I see his smile, hear his laughter, feel his arms around me. Then, as though he is a ghost who has just walked through my bedroom wall, the memory is gone.

I still wonder how he would look now, who would he have married, how many children he would have had. I grieve for the daughter-in-law and the grandchildren I will never know. Time has not eased what I will never know or crave, for no parent should ever suffer barren arms. There isn't a day I don't yearn to have Christopher back.

I would give my life for his and there isn't a moment I don't wish that I could wind back the clock, be given a second chance. There isn't a day when I don't sit in my rocking chair on our front verandah overlooking Christopher's garden and tell him how much I love and miss him.

And sometimes at night, Phil and I will sit together with a glass of wine and ask each other what happened—how did it all go so terribly wrong? There is no answer in silence.

And finally, after eleven years, I have stopped searching for one. I had to let Christopher go, for him and for me. I don't know for certain if he exists in another spiritual realm but, for a time, I felt him near me and that was all that mattered when I had given up on living. Now, I talk to him every day—just in case. There is much I don't understand but I know this; life doesn't end with the heart's last beat.

We went back to the headland on the eleventh anniversary—just Phil and me. We sat in the pre-dawn dark on the grass verge, under Christopher's floodlight and at the exact spot where, 10 metres below, his life ended. We huddled and waited for the new day to begin.

Then with arms outstretched, the yellow orb of the dawning sun throbbed in time to the burgeoning orchestral cacophony of nature. It burst through the horizontal hymen with a glint and, with a curtsy, danced off to its own tune. The subservient ocean dazzled in shimmering strobes, beckoning with tiny, encouraging fingers of mirrored light.

A sailboat rocked in the distance and surfers bobbed on the undulating tide. Soon joggers and dogs and seagulls and swimmers and fishermen and mothers and fathers and children with buckets and spades would rush to this pretty beach to build another memory. They won't look up to see the middle-aged couple holding hands on the precipice, looking out to sea, their features faded, expressions altered by the deep gashes of time and grief. They won't see the lovers they used to be or their silent acceptance that renders them slaves to an uncertain future. They won't hear the laments—never spoken, never said, but just enough to disturb their sleep.

For this is where we stand—Phil and I—alone at future's gate. We can shake it or turn the key.

The last inspirational card from Christopher's diary reads:

> Life is about making choices. Make it and try. Focus on making it happen. Never give up. My peace is a great gift to the world—when I find my peace, there is one less person suffering.

Afterword
Gordon Parker

The phone rang at home as I was getting out of the shower. An ominous early morning call, held off until daylight. It was Jayne. She apologised before stating quietly and tensely, 'Chris died last night.'

Died. Perhaps a car accident? I tried to keep the urgency out of my voice but asked 'how' almost immediately. At one level, irrelevant, as the death of an adolescent is an enormity in and of itself.

Jayne reported that Chris had fallen down the Avalon headlands. He had become separated from friends, dropped his mobile phone over the cliffs and apparently slipped trying to retrieve it.

Please, not suicide, I thought. For many health professionals the suicide of a depressed patient is *the* marker of their greatest failure. Failure to relieve their patient's distress, failure to instil hope that life is worth living and failure to assist the patient to recognise that their depression will improve and pass. Failure. Learning of a suicide starts immediate self-questioning, a review of possible acts of commission and of omission—perhaps something said or, conversely, failure to act during a high-risk period.

As the day went on I knew that misadventure was an unsustainable explanation. I contacted the psychologist who had been helping me manage Chris over several months, and who reported that Chris had texted a distressed message on the day of his death but had appeared reassured by some suggestions returned by text. Driving to the Newlings' house that evening I replayed an image only a few months old.

Of a Saturday afternoon rugby match at Northbridge, at Shore's playing fields which were dedicated to its so many boys who had lost their lives in the First and Second World Wars at the height of their youth. The Shore and Scots First XV teams were playing on the main oval. A scrum ruptured and I glimpsed a Shore boy dive explosively at the instigator and land a dextrous uppercut before the referee could blow his whistle. It was Chris. An impetuous detonation I'd never seen from him before and one rarely observed by his family. For anyone who is suicidal, a propensity for precipitous action can be one of the most worrying factors, as it can summarily override any self-protective strategies.

I called up an image of Chris on the Avalon headland. Perhaps further disinhibited by alcohol, perhaps going blazingly into the night with a 'fuck it all' detonation of emotions—overriding logic and the love of his family and his many friends.

But an image is not an explanation. As Kay Redfield Jamison—a distinguished psychologist colleague and author of the wonderfully evocative book *An Unquiet Mind*—observed in a later book, 'An act against the self, suicide is also a violent force in the lives of the others. It is incomprehensible when it kills the young.'[1] In that book Jamison sketched her own suicidal mood states as background to a comprehensive and academic overview of suicide. Her book has a quite differing emphasis to Jayne's account but the two complement each other and provide the richest and most evocative writings on suicide of which I'm aware, and I will therefore interleave some of Jamison's observations in my discussion here.

As often occurs following a suicide—and even more when involving an adolescent—diverse explanations and facts emerge, evolve and sometimes remain ever incomplete and incomprehensible. Jayne has vividly described their home that evening: everyone enveloped by grief and impotence in the immediate 'impact phase'. A narrative was being consolidated. One of Chris's friends had seen him slip on the rocks as he tried to collect his mobile phone. A construction of misadventure—of a fateful slip—and one that might ease the alternative, the enormity of a suicide. But a girlfriend's statement to the police led an officer to inform Jayne gently but bluntly—'*If it's an accident the person calls out. A suicide, they never do. There was no scream, Mrs Newling.*'

Time has allowed pieces of that alternative explanation to be collected. In her scarifying account of Chris's last day, Jayne details many stressful precursors: his high intake of alcohol, his being at the headland for some time before being found by friends—with one texting another that Chris was talking about suicide and that he had broken the car mirror and thrown it and his mobile phone down the cliff. We can presume he had a plan: the drive to the headland, then phases of contemplation and agitation before a combustible flame of untempered and impulsive emotions. Thus, seemingly, not as precipitous as I had imagined and, as I read Jayne's account, I went back into morbid self-questioning.

It is not uncommon for people committed to killing themselves to spend time in contemplation at the site in what is known as a 'suicidal mode', with Jamison stating that 'ambivalence saturates the suicidal act'.[2] At such times, most are agitated but some almost frozen, and such behaviours may alert astute observers. In the 1960s, a tavern owner at Watsons Bay in Sydney had a German shepherd dog named Rexie who could sense if someone was contemplating jumping from the cliffs at The Gap, an infamous Sydney suicide hotspot. Rexie would start barking and run to the edge of the cliffs, allowing time for others to intervene, and it was estimated that the dog saved about thirty lives. The late Don Ritchie who lived adjacent to The Gap would walk slowly towards someone he judged at risk, strike up a conversation and invite them to come to his home for a cup of tea and a chat. Over nearly fifty years it was estimated that he saved several hundred lives. Don supported the Black Dog Institute's collaboration with the local council in redressing the high risks posed by The Gap; in addition to fencing, it now has CCTV coverage to help identify those who are clearly distressed and at risk. I have even wondered if we could train the equivalent of 'life savers' as a further safeguard. Another example of an effective 'detector' is of the highway patrol policeman who patrolled the Golden Gate Bridge in San Francisco. When he presciently observed someone at risk, he would park his bike a distance away, stroll slowly to the suicidal person, introduce himself, invite the suicidal individual to join him for a coffee and, by asking 'What are your plans for tomorrow?', would move the distressed individual's thinking from the perturbing present to the future.

If only. If only someone with such skills had been there that night, to talk Chris down. But he did have friends there, genuinely and fearfully concerned, and they were clearly alert to the high-risk scenario. An adolescent's peer groups generally dictate key decisions, but Chris broke away from them and their support—and here we can presume a precipitous decision, driven by psychological pain and disinhibited by alcohol. Few depressed people who contemplate or attempt suicide do so because they want to die—for most, they simply want the pain to stop. His friends search for him down at the beach. Chris is observed two-thirds up the cliff and then falling. As Jayne writes in a later chapter, 'For Christopher, it was easier to let go than to hold on'. Earlier she observes even more poignantly, 'No one should die alone and in fear.'

'If only' a Rexie or a Don Ritchie had been there then it might have been different. But I suspect during that high-risk period Chris moved into an impervious non-negotiation zone. As observed by Jamison: 'For those with a short wick ... and impulse-laden wiring ... it is as though the nervous system has been soaked in kerosene [and one or more precipitants] ignite a suicidal response'.[3] As Jayne writes, 'There was a moment, an impulsive second where death was desirable.' And, here lies the heart of the tragedy, a moment experienced by so many people was acted on with irrevocable consequences.

As Jamison observes, family members 'are left to deal with the guilt and the anger ... to try to understand an inexplicable act ... to miss a child whose life was threaded to theirs from its very beginning' and so, in the context of those who are left behind, the suicidal act appears 'personal, cruel and thoughtless ... yet suicide is tangential to reason and ... is almost always an irrational choice, the seemingly best way to end the pain, the futility or ... the hopelessness'.[4]

An even greater tragedy when suicidal thinking is generally a temporary state. One of the few people to survive jumping off the Golden Gate Bridge was interviewed almost immediately afterwards by a journalist, who asked what his thoughts were when he was halfway down. The survivor smiled and stated, 'I realised that I had three problems in my life currently but that two were correctible.' In essence, suicide is a tragically permanent solution to a temporary problem. That reality should underpin our plans to reduce predisposing risks but also our approach to those periods of high risk.

As a professional my brief was to identify and ease Chris's pain. We first met in August 2001 when Chris was sixteen and suspended from school for smoking cigarettes and marijuana. My priorities as an assessing psychiatrist are to identify the particular condition (i.e. provide a diagnosis), select the most appropriate treatment paradigm and craft a management plan. Such tasks are common across all age groups but adolescents bring other issues to the foreground. Adolescence itself is a stressor—some of the many issues that need to be faced include moving to a more independent life stage, preoccupation with physical appearance and identity, peer group pressures (including bullying), handling home life, school strictures and examinations, contemplating career options, and making choices about drugs, alcohol and sex. Add a substantive mood disorder, plus perceived stigma associated with the need to attend a professional, and the adolescent is further weighed down. Australia has led the way in advancing the destigmatising of depression but until mood disorders can be viewed and discussed as comfortably as medical problems, there is still a considerable dissonance, with such stigma experienced more severely by adolescents.

Chris appeared comfortable about assessment. He related well, and in between periods of clear despair, his baseline sunny and mischievous personality style shone through before a worried mien would return to create shadows. He detailed a strong history of depression in the family but I positioned his depression as secondary to other factors, especially when the disorder had failed to respond to an antidepressant prescribed by his excellent general practitioner John Eccles. I judged the primary problem as a set of anxiety disorders present since early childhood, which had worsened when Chris developed a severe and prolonged infection at three years of age and with the anxiety becoming increasingly debilitating in adolescence. Regrettably, he was handling it by self-medication, with the marijuana and alcohol creating their own problems. It was clear that rugby was his key priority and sporting success integral to his identity. However, his leg muscles had not grown at the same rate as his leg bones, and depite a number of surgical procedures none had produced any definitive improvement. He was in considerable pain, especially when he exercised and, perhaps worse, he was pessimistic that the medical and physiotherapy interventions would correct the increasing limitations and pain that dogged every training session and match. I doubt whether his coaches or team companions had any appreciation of just how much pain he was experiencing and how he sought to push himself through the pain barrier. This was a mark of his courage but also of his desperate concern to maintain and advance his identity as an elite rugby player, and he saw that aspiration melting away. Loss of that role and its potential in the future struck me as central and shaped discussions with the Shore authorities as to how it might be addressed practically. As noted by Jayne, the forethought, wisdom and practical pastoral care brought to addressing this issue by headmaster Bob Grant and school counsellor John Burns were exemplary, sensitive and demonstrated that the school authorities 'walked the walk' and did not merely 'talk the talk' of pastoral care.

Management strategies also involved modifications to medication and referral to a psychologist to address his significant anxiety states. However, review sessions suggested that therapeutic gains were slight, either reflecting their intrinsic failure to gain traction and/or background issues—of living arrangements, his girlfriend, and drugs and alcohol. These latter issues remained in the background, perhaps reflecting their peripheral status or the private world of his adolescence. As the months went by, my initial respect for Chris and his courage increased further. When the shadows of depression disappeared intermittently from his face, I could observe more of his intrinsic personality as described so evocatively in Jayne's account. The tragic death of any adolescent evokes a flood of grief throughout their family and community but, as detailed by Jayne, Chris's death had an immense impact. The memorial service at Shore brought an extraordinary number of people, overflowing across the lawns from the chapel. Headmaster Grant asked me the day before to sit with him and his wife during the service. I appreciated such sensitivity—it partially salved my personal sense of failure to bring his depression under control and his parents' unstated expectations of keeping him alive—it signalled a team effort. I observed the line of silent, solemn and preoccupied masters, with several struggling to contain their distress, who became an informal guard of honour as people left the chapel. Jayne recounts the impact of Chris's death on those beyond the family, his closest friends and his rugby teammates who played above themselves in a memorial match, and the many who tattooed themselves to forever cement their memories of him. Such an outpouring not only speaks of how he was viewed but of the reality that the loss of those who enrich life is felt so keenly and for so long.

As many have observed, depression is the core and key driver of suicidality and thus bringing the mood disorder under control and into remission is the objective. Depression alone can be borne 'as long as there is the belief that things will improve', writes Jamison. 'If that belief cracks or disappears, suicide becomes the option of choice.'[5]

CLINICAL DEPRESSION IN ADOLESCENTS

The teenage years are marked by emotional swings and where depressed 'moods' are normal. In an earlier book, my co-author Kerrie Eyers and I sought to nominate features differentiating 'clinical' depression from 'normal' depression, although acknowledging that no one feature is absolute.[6] While depression is itself defined by a drop in self-esteem and a rise in self-criticism, clinical depression is reflected in more dimensionally extreme plummets into feelings of worthlessness and numbness and the belief that life is not worth living. Other candidate features (and principally ones indicating 'melancholia'—the biological expression of clinical depression) are becoming 'asocial' (not mixing with friends or, of more concern, not responding to their mobile phone calls and texts), remaining in their room, lacking energy to get out of bed or even bathe, losing the light in their eyes, not reacting to pleasurable events and seemingly not able to be cheered up (other than superficially or temporarily), experiencing distinct changes in appetite and sleep, having impaired concentration, and being physically slowed down or agitated. A significant minority will be extremely irritable, angry and volatile. The gravity of the state is increased if it persists.

Bipolar mood disorders appear increasingly prevalent in adolescents. Such conditions are marked by oscillations in mood states from depressions to 'highs' (or 'mania/hypomania'), with the individual full of verve and zest in those latter states. At such times, the adolescent is highly energised (often childishly playful), overtalkative to loud, sleeping less if not minimally—but not tired. Their day-to-day worries disappear and they feel bulletproof and invulnerable, often highly creative, and become verbally and socially indiscrete—with their high libido and disinhibition, and perhaps driving faster, drinking more (and often less likely to appear intoxicated), and buying unneeded or unaffordable clothes. Such states may last hours to months, are usually followed by a sense of shame about activities engaged in and, as the mood can drop precipitously from a high into a melancholic depression (remembered by the adolescent as a 'black hole' of despair), the suicide risk is high—the suicide rate for bipolar II disorder (the bipolar type where the individual is not psychotic during the 'highs') exceeds all other psychiatric conditions.

CANDIDATE SUICIDE RISK SCENARIOS

As noted, those with a bipolar II condition and experiencing a rapid drop from a hypomanic 'high' manic to a melancholic state are at high risk of suicide. For those with a melancholic depression the risk is present during the episode but a time of increased risk is as the individual is emerging from their depression and, being more energised, is more likely and able to act on their suicidal preoccupations. In one study conducted by Jamison, one-third of hospitalised patients looked normal to 'their doctors, family members or friends in the minutes or hours just before suicide'.[7] For those with non-biological mood disorders, certain life-event stressors alone, or in conjunction with the adolescent's personality, may fuel suicidal thinking and acts. For example, demeaning stressors such as being bullied, being rejected by a partner or even by the adolescent's peer group or being dismissed unfairly at work can induce suicidal thinking by their 'meaning' to the adolescent as well as by their acuteness. We can all generally adjust to chronic stressors but we are much more likely to be perturbed by stressors with an acute onset and a demeaning impact, and particularly if they induce a sense of hopelessness.

Over-represented personality styles include traits of perfectionism—as the adolescent sets such high standards and over-reacts to any perceived failure to achieve a goal, while they also lack the flexibility to concede that there is always a third option rather than 'bust through or bust'. Those with a personality style hypersensitive to judgement by others—and particularly to abandonment and rejection—and those with a 'short fuse' are also more likely to put themselves at suicidal risk.

Any at-risk period is clearly advanced by easy access to the means to commit the act, any glorifying of suicide (with the suicide of an adolescent's idol provoking a 'copy cat' phenomenon), the adolescent having friends or peers who have killed themself (leading to so-called 'cluster suicides'), and disinhibiting drugs and alcohol. 'Substance abuse loads the cylinder with more bullets,' Jamison explains. 'By acting to disinhibit behaviour, drugs and alcohol increase risk-taking, violence and impulsivity. For those who are suicidal ... this may be lethal.'[8]

CHALLENGES TO SOME MYTHS SURROUNDING ADOLESCENT SUICIDE

- Suicidal thinking is not that rare in adolescents. Jamison reported several US studies of school and college students, with some 50 per cent having suicidal thoughts, some 20 per cent seriously considering killing themselves in the preceding twelve months and 16 per cent of those having drawn up a plan.[9]

- If an adolescent attempts but survives suicide, many people judge that it was simply an attempt and the adolescent would not have followed through, or view talking about suicide as 'just talk'. Not so. Adolescents who commit suicide are distinctly more likely to have made previous attempts (and to have self-harmed) and to have communicated their intention or preoccupation. So-called 'cries for help' should be recognised as just that—and not simply as an attention-seeking strategy.
- Conversely, some people believe that if an individual has attempted suicide, they will inevitably kill themself by a future attempt. One researcher traced 515 people who had been restrained from jumping off the Golden Gate Bridge. Decades later only 6 per cent of these individuals had killed themselves or died in circumstances suggestive of suicide.[10]
- Some parents and even mental health professionals believe that seeking promises or drawing up contracts will prevent the adolescent from attempting suicide. While an adolescent might genuinely commit to the plan at the time, it has little holding power in itself if the adolescent returns to a suicidal mood. As such 'contracts' have no binding power and can offer a false sense of relief, they should neither be negotiated nor trusted.
- While all professionals will check at appropriate times about suicide risk, denials may not be valid and often the professional must proceed by their 'instinct' or by indirect appraisal. This reality holds for adults as well. As observed by Jamison: 'Suicide is not beholden to an evening's promises, nor does it always hearken to plans drawn up in lucid moments and banked in good intentions.'[11]
- Professionals are not very accurate in judging the risk of suicide with a number of studies establishing that their capacity to

predict is comparable to that of intelligent non-professionals. The lack of such skill largely reflects the low prevalence of actual suicide in those at risk. Of any ten adolescents that I might judge as being at high risk over a year, and requiring close attention, contingency plans and even hospitalisation, only one might remain in that high-risk category after a year. Thus, while we can retrospectively analyse the individual factors that may have caused an adolescent to suicide, our prospective capacity to predict is quite limited.

- Adolescent suicides are not currently increasing in Australia. Suicide rates vary considerably across the decades, across age bands (being second highest in Australia in those aged 15–19) and across regions and countries (Australia is mid-range), and reflect a range of socio-cultural determinants (e.g. unemployment, rural and remote communities) and protective or therapeutic strategies. An Australian report quantified that suicide had declined in males aged 20–24 from 40 in 100 000 males in 1997–98 (when Australia's National Suicide Prevention Strategy was initiated), to 20 in 100 000 in 2003.[12] While we cannot become complacent—as every suicide is a tragedy and suicide is the leading cause of death in the 15–24 age band— the situation is improving and is likely to reflect a number of factors. A key factor, I believe, is the destigmatisation of mood disorders in Australia. This has succeeded beyond expectations and so encouraged young people to seek support from their friends and, in particular, to be more prepared to seek and obtain professional help. Effective preventative programs have been initiated by a large number of organisations and Helen Christensen is currently developing internet-based suicide

prevention programs at the Black Dog Institute that feature psychological strategies, distraction interventions and crisis planning.
- While antidepressant medication has been shown in large trials to increase the risk of suicidal thoughts and attempts by about 2 per cent, such medication use is associated with a decreased rather than an increased rate of completed youth suicide.

REDUCING THE RISK OF ADOLESCENT SUICIDE—A CLINICAL PERSPECTIVE

Jamison writes: 'Together, doctors, patients, and their family members can minimise the chance of suicide, but it is a difficult, subtle, and frustrating venture. Its value is obvious, but the ways of achieving it are not. Anyone who suggests that coming back from suicidal despair is a straightforward journey has never taken it.'[13]

While prevention spans socio-cultural, economic and other domains in addition to the psychological state of the adolescent, a few clinical principles are offered for consideration. As noted, all adolescents experience depressed times but, if there is the possibility of a clinical mood disorder and/or if the individual is exposed to high-risk scenarios, a parent should seek professional help, whether it be from a school counsellor, a general practitioner or a mental health professional, and if their management or advice seems ineffective, transfer management to another professional. In our book *Navigating Teenage Depression* we detailed what a parent should expect of a professional assessment.

About the maintenance of confidentiality, while many professionals disallow any contact between themselves and the parents, I do not believe such a position is sustainable. Ideally, the depressed or troubled adolescent will agree for the professional to provide some initial and subsequent feedback to the parents (after the therapist has checked with the adolescent about what should remain confidential) and management should effectively be a 'team game'. This may involve the professional working with the adolescent but, at the end of the session and with the adolescent in the room, allowing the parent to add their observations and to tweak management nuances.

The professional should accept urgent or emergency calls from parents rather than regard the therapeutic arena as sacrosanct to the adolescent and themself. In such instances, the professional should act as a 'receiver' (to the concerns raised by the parent) but is not required to act as a 'transmitter' (i.e. discussing what the adolescent has raised with them). The last is, in my view, overridden if the adolescent is at high risk, where I believe it is not only appropriate for the parent to be contacted and options for proceeding discussed but may be mandatory. An admission to a psychiatric hospital may be extremely stigmatising to an adolescent and distressing at the time but, again, in my view, it is preferable to be overprotective rather than laissez-faire. Perhaps, more importantly, it is rare in my experience for an adolescent to criticise their practitioner for so acting after they have been discharged from hospital.

Other strategies include media and school education, restricting access to means of self-harm, training 'gatekeepers' (e.g. teachers) who will recognise and respond to those at risk, and—of key impact—awareness of crisis support services such as Lifeline, Kids Helpline and the Suicide Call Back Service. Suicide Prevention Australia (www.suicidepreventionaust.org) has prepared informative reports that address this priority area practically, sensitively and with much wise advice.

THE FALLACY OF 'MOVING ON'

Of the many points and lessons we can assemble from Jayne's heart-wrenching account, one in particular is that when speaking with a parent whose child has killed themselves, we should shun the question (implicit or explicit) as to whether they have 'moved on', or, perhaps even more insensitively, indicate that it is time for them to 'move on'. There is, in my view, no finite period of grief, and I cannot imagine any parent ever completely moving on from the death of their child. Bert Facey, the Australian writer of *A Fortunate Life*, described a childhood of sadistic abuse and deprivation, and an adult life marked by privation, losses, unrelenting labour and horrors—the last including his time at Gallipoli in World War 1. Yet, in his simply written and compassionate book, he regarded himself as 'fortunate', with reviewers emphasising his tranquillity of spirit, equanimity and absence of recrimination about all those who exploited him. There was only one event that Facey judged that he never overcame—the death of his son in the Battle of Singapore in World War 2.[14]

When a child has killed themself there is—as experienced by Jayne and Phil—an extra dimension to the grief experienced by parents. The world of 'if only': 'What if we had done X or not done Y?' Most feel that they had failed in their role as parents—to provide a safe harbour, to raise their child to adulthood and, commonly, because they weren't 'there' for their child in those final hours or minutes.

These strictures are unique to parental grief and do not come from depression, which intriguingly can have benefits over time. We reported a survey of patients attending the Black Dog Institute Depression Clinic and with most currently still 'on the journey' of dealing with their mood disorder. When asked the Stephen Fry question: 'If there was a button that, if pressed, would remove your mood disorder, would you press it?' twenty two per cent of those with a depressive condition and 62 per cent with a bipolar disorder stated that they would still choose to have their mood disorder.[15] Offered reasons included that in knowing pain they had learned more how to experience joy and they had developed greater empathy. They had learned to appreciate (and not take for granted) the days when the sun was shining, they had cut out negative people and negative influences from their lives, they were kinder to themselves, they re-evaluated their goals and changed their life priorities, and had developed a new self-respect and compassion for themselves. They could pace themselves better during fresh episodes, operating to the mantra 'This too will pass'.[16]

By contrast, grief for a parent has no redeeming features. While it will not pass, it will ease over time. As a crisis, it makes the parent more subject to change—as it is a rare individual who changes when life is proceeding without a crisis. For many, the change can be for the worse or initiate a cascade of negative consequences and events. Parents are far more likely to separate; grief may be drowned in alcohol or expressed across a range of self-destructive acts.

Suicide of a child increases all such risks. Jamison judges that suicide is 'a death like no other, and those who are left behind to struggle with it must confront a pain like no other. They are left with the shock and the unending 'what ifs'. They are left with anger and guilt... to a bank of questions, both asked and unasked, about why; they are left to the silence of others, who are horrified, embarrassed, or unable to cobble together a note of condolence, an embrace, or a comment; and they are left with an assumption by others—and themselves—that more could have been done.' She adds: 'It rips apart lives and beliefs, and it sets its survivors on a prolonged and devastating journey ... of having failed the child at the most critical time of his life, of being insensitive to the extent of his pain, or of overlooking final cues.'[17]

Can we find—or speculate—that the death of Chris has led to changes in the lives of the Newling family and others who experienced its impact? Let me gratuitously suggest several. Jayne is clearly a superb writer—that latent ability may never have been brought to full fruition otherwise—and she has produced a book that will be accorded 'classic' status. She has elected to work in palliative care and it would be hard not to imagine that her grief has not brought an additional understanding to her intrinsic empathy. Both she and husband Phil now have a deeper understanding of each other and of their bond. All Chris's friends will have a greater appreciation of the tenuous nature of life and its immanent risks. For some, it will have decreased the chance of them being victims of alcohol and drugs, some will have grown up more quickly and matured more rapidly, and some might therefore have reset feckless life priorities to substantive ones. These are all speculative musings, but there is one consequence where Chris's death led to a calling for his brother Nic that is enduring and almost beyond comprehension.

NIC NEWLING
Nic was referred to me in 2001 when he was fifteen. As recorded by Jayne he had been awarded an academic scholarship to Shore and additionally was an accomplished actor in school productions. At thirteen, however, he developed a gravid mood disorder, marked by delusions and hallucinations as well as mood swings and severe anxiety attacks. At fourteen, he was beset by intrusive

suicidal preoccupations. An expert in anxiety disorders diagnosed anxiety and initiated hypnotherapy, an expert in obsessive compulsive disorder diagnosed OCD, while an expert in schizophrenia diagnosed schizophrenia. In consequence, Nic was hospitalised for ten months in an inpatient psychiatric unit and prescribed multiple antidepressant and antipsychotic medications.

My initial assessment of Nic identified relatively distinct 'highs' as well as depressive episodes and I favoured a bipolar disorder diagnosis. Nic had great difficulty getting to school and when he did (usually once a week), his mood and markedly impaired concentration led to him generally spending the day in the sick room. Numerous investigations were undertaken and I sought the views of a number of other experts in Sydney and also one in the United States, both to clarify diagnostic nuances and to consider possible treatment options after he had been unable to benefit from so many differing classes of psychotropic medications.

Despite the gravity of his condition, there was something about Nic. He had the maturity of a wise adult, his questioning of options and management nuances was extraordinarily sophisticated and, when the light came to his eyes, the pre-morbid intelligent, creative and bantering Nic was a joy. We knew—and he had a superb counsellor and later an equally superb psychologist—that if we could keep him alive, he would one day flower.

His last few years at school were all the more difficult because he had fallen behind academically and lost his peer group as they proceeded to their HSC year—despite Shore providing exceptional support. His father reported a weight being lifted from his shoulders when Nic left school, went to work in Phil's office and began to rebuild the company's website. He had also been accepted into a drama course. By 2003, he and his parents felt that he had 'turned the corner'.

In 2007 I was asked to give a talk on mood disorders in adolescents at a conference for school principals at Barker College. Nic had stated previously that, as a consequence of his experience and Chris's death, he wanted to contribute to educational programs. At Barker I gave an 'outside in' overview of mood disorders—somewhat academic and risking sterility—and was followed by Nic who gave a complementary 'inside out' view of his personal journey. I'm competitive—speaking gigs included—but I was completely outclassed by the 21-year-old neophyte Nic. Later as we sat at the official table, so many principals came to compliment him, with one (who had probably never publicly admitted any fallibility) saying: 'Nic, thank you. I should add that I have walked in your shoes.' I received a note from his parents reporting his keen pleasure and I record here part of my rather earnest response: 'I have always felt that he will do something special in life and I am starting to get some embryonic sense of his unique capacity to communicate at a quite exceptional level. Where it will manifest itself in the future (theatre or whatever) is unpredictable now but it will be somewhere.'

As Nic became an advocate for advancing the understanding of mood disorders and suicide in adolescents—relating his personal story openly, wryly and whimsically—his mood disorder settled further; medications were able to be reduced, and we set the objective of no medications in the future. I have learned over the years that those who develop severe bipolar disorders at a young age generally improve the most. In addition, those who speak about their mood disorder (and Australia has been blessed by many such high-profile politicians and sportspeople) develop a level of invulnerability. In speaking openly, they are no longer at the centre of a secret. I have never heard anyone criticise those brave enough to tell their personal stories.

In 2007, Nic's mood swings were under good control; he had rejoined 'life', and he embarked on a delayed Gap year. He was working part-time in IT, socialising and engaging in comedy performances. In 2008 he was employed in a highly sought-after IT position and by 2010 his psychologist (David Gilfillan) and I could gradually withdraw. I seek to make a key point here. Those reading Jayne's account of Nic's highly disturbed psychotic world in adolescence may feel that such murky forces simply lie latent, waiting to emerge later. Any such concern needs to be firmly redressed to guard against any misinterpretation by readers. Nic's psychotic world disappeared. It will not return.

In 2011 Nic commenced work at the Black Dog Institute. Here he has taken key responsibility for its website for adolescents, called BITE BACK, demonstrating his extraordinary creativity and empathy, and building on his personal experience. Since then I've become aware of the people he has helped—over social media and in real-life high-risk situations, though I didn't learn this from Nic himself, as he is extremely modest and self-effacing and perhaps even oblivious to some of his skills. But—and here is the central message—not only has he brought hope to so many young people in despair, I'm aware that he has directly saved the lives of several young adolescents. Whether all of this would have occurred if Chris had lived is, in my view, doubtful, though noting this is somewhat risky. I'm providing details about an ex-patient and, while I have the approval and permission of Nic and his parents, there will be many professionals who will view writing about him as a boundary violation or even exploitation. I hope they are wrong for, if we are to destigmatise mood disorders, inspiring personal stories—subject to appropriate checks and balances—should advance that agenda. A more salient risk is that in so many of us recording our admiration for Nic, it may put extra pressure on him to continue the task. His work with mental health may be a calling in life; however, this does not mean that it must continue as Nic's only focus or goal. The path of his life is his choice alone to make.

Jamison observed: 'The suffering of the suicidal is private and inexpressible, leaving family members, friends, and colleagues to deal with an almost unfathomable kind of loss, as well as guilt. Suicide carries in its aftermath a level of confusion and devastation that is, for the most part, beyond description.'[18] Later she records a military chaplain: 'I do not know why young men have to die. You would think it would break the heart of God.'[19] But then she adds a wry observation by one man: 'We can't put it all in God's hands. God's busy.'[20]

Jamison finished her book with an excerpt from a poem by Douglas Dunn and noted the fragment (which she kept on her desk) that had drawn her back to life—'Look to the living, love them, and hold on.'[21] It is a mantra for those at risk of suicide and it may also be a mantra for those who survive the suicide of a relative—but then perhaps only able to be approached after an extended period and by those—like the Newlings—who possess the capacity to truly love.

Jayne Newling has taken us into a very private domain and provided us with a harrowing description that is exceptional in its rawness, openness, honesty and insights. Her 'inked memories of what might have been' will be etched on all who read this classic.

missing christopher

Gordon Parker AO is Scientia Professor of Psychiatry at the University of New South Wales, Professorial Fellow at the Black Dog Institute and a renowned researcher and expert on mood disorders. He is co-editor with Kerrie Eyers and Tessa Wigney of the bestselling book *Journeys with the Black Dog*, and co-author with Kerrie Eyers of *Navigating Teenage Depression*. He has written many other books on depression and mood disorders, including *Dealing with Depression*. His autobiography, *A Piece of My Mind*, was published in 2012.

ENDNOTES

1. Kay Redfield Jamison, *Night Falls Fast*, Picador, London 2000, p. 18
2. *Night Falls Fast*, p. 39
3. *Night Falls Fast*, p. 197
4. *Night Falls Fast*, pp. 291–2
5. *Night Falls Fast*, p. 94
6. Gordon Parker and Kerrie Eyers, *Navigating Teenage Depression*, Allen & Unwin, Sydney 2009
7. *Night Falls Fast*, p. 115
8. *Night Falls Fast*, p. 127
9. *Night Falls Fast*, p. 37
10. Richard H. Seiden, 'Where Are They Now? A Follow-up Study of Suicide Attempters from the Golden Gate Bridge', Suicide and Life-Threatening Behavior, 1978, vol. 8, no. 4, pp. 203–16
11. *Night Falls Fast*, p. 5
12. Stephen Morrell, Andrew N. Page, Richard J. Taylor, 'The decline in Australian young male suicide', *Social Science and Medicine*, 2007, vol. 64, no. 3, pp. 747–54
13. *Night Falls Fast*, p. 236
14. Albert Facey, *A Fortunate Life*, 1988, Penguin, Ringwood, Vic. 1988
15. Gordon Parker, Amelia Paterson, Kathryn Fletcher, Bianca Blanch, et al. 'The "magic button question" for those with a mood disorder—Would they wish to re-live their condition?', *Journal of Affective Disorders*, 2012, vol. 136, no. 3, pp. 419–24
16. Tessa Wigney, Kerrie Eyers, Gordon Parker (eds), *Journeys with the Black Dog*, Allen & Unwin, Sydney 2007
17. *Night Falls Fast*, p. 295
18. *Night Falls Fast*, p. 24
19. *Night Falls Fast*, p. 69
20. *Night Falls Fast*, p. 289
21. From Douglas Dunn, 'Disenchantments', quoted in *Night Falls Fast*, p. 311

Acknowledgements

I would like to extend my thanks to the following people:

To my parents Tom and Ellie, Phil's parents, Graham and Moya, and to our brothers and sisters and extended family—thank you for your love and support.

To our dear friends, Daisy and Mandy Richards, Trish Murgatroyd, Mel Steers and Pauline McMahon, who held our hands and protected us through all the difficult times. In their own special way they all helped us survive the early shock and trauma of Christopher's death and continue to do so.

To Christopher's friends who loved and supported us and who honour him on each and every anniversary of his death. A special thanks to Ben 'Murgy' Murgatroyd who is still a major part of our lives.

To Zach for making me laugh and for teaching me how to love again and to Sarah for trusting me and giving me unfettered access to indulge my beautiful grandson.

To Ashleigh: thank you—and you were right to throw out the clock.

To Angie Moore for her love, care and insight and for helping me to realise it wasn't my fault.

A special thank you to our family doctor, John Eccles, who with great compassion helped me to understand what really happened that night at the headland.

To my brother-in-law, cinematographer Allen Koppe, who gave me the greatest gift of all, the beautiful photograph of Christopher when he was happy.

Thanks to Patti Miller and my fellow Faber Academy writers for their enduring kindness, patience and encouragement during chapter readings.

A huge thanks to Sophia Barnes, editor and manuscript assessor and my very first reader who gave me the confidence to seek publication instead of filing the pages in a drawer. To my other readers, whose detailed and complimentary feedback made me realise I had a story in which others would be interested—Will Bonney, Robin Bell, Amelia Paterson, Kate Fagan, Josie Harris, Jo Wise and Dan Harris.

Thanks to the incredible team at Allen & Unwin: publisher Elizabeth Weiss, editor Ann Lennox and copyeditor Susin Chow.

Thank you to Robert Grant AM, John Burns, Graham Robertson, Matthew Pickering and Antony Weiss for everything they did for Christopher and my family. Also to the greater Shore community who kept us fed in a far greater way than Trish or I could ever manage or imagine.

I want to thank the team at the Black Dog Institute: Executive Director Helen Christensen, Chairman Peter Joseph AM, General Manager Will Bonney and Kerrie Eyers AM.

A very deep and special thanks to Professor Gordon Parker AO, founder of the Black Dog Institute. When Sophia encouraged me to seek publication, I sent the manuscript to Gordon for his permission to use his name and that of the Institute. He not only gave his personal endorsement but offered to write an afterword in honour of Christopher and our family. He reassured Phil and me that it is normal to expect that our pain will ease but also told us to expect that it will last a lifetime. I always knew that it was never okay to ask 'are you over it yet?', to say that 'time heals' or 'it's time to move on', but I've always felt guilty that I couldn't be the person I was before Christopher died. Gordon has made me realise I don't have to be. I thank him for his integrity, insight and for his unstinting support of my family over the past eleven years. But most importantly, Phil and I thank him not only for saving Nic but for giving him his life back.